Legends of the West Publishing Co.
Publisher of From Slave to Superstar of the Wild West

Tom DeMund
Publisher

174 Santa Rosa Avenue
Sausalito, CA 94965
Orders: (800) 852-4890
Phone: (415) 331-2516
FAX: (415) 331-0532
E-mail: legendsofthew@aol.com
legendsofthewestpublishing.com

From Slave to
Superstar
of the Wild West

From Slave to Superstar *of the* Wild West

THE AWESOME STORY OF JIM BECKWOURTH

Portrait of Jim Beckwourth

Tom DeMund

Legends of the West Publishing Company
Sausalito, California

Published by: Legends of the West Publishing Company
174 Santa Rosa Avenue
Sausalito, California 94965

Front cover: Photo of statuette of Jim Beckwourth, courtesy of Laura Root from her series "All God's Children," Martha Root Originals, the Beckwourth cabin and old log corral, Beckwourth, California, and Beckwourth Peak in the background.

Title page: Portrait of Jim Beckwourth by C. Waldo Love, painted between 1930 and 1939 from an earlier photo, courtesy of the Denver Historical Society.

Cover design: Pete Masterson, Aeonix Publishing Group, www.aeonix.com
Interior design: Joan Olson
Editing: Zipporah W. Collins

All color photographs and maps are by the author and his wife, Mary, except the aerial photographs on pages 59, 114, and 124, which are by Woodward Payne.

Publisher's Cataloging-in-Publication Data
DeMund, Tom.
From slave to superstar of the wild west : the awesome story of Jim Beckwourth / by Tom DeMund.
p. cm.
Includes bibliographical references and index.
ISBN-10: 0-9786904-0-0
ISBN-13: 978–0-9786904-0-3
[1. Beckwourth, James Pierson, 1798–1866. 2. Frontier and pioneer life—West (U.S.) 3. Trappers—West (U.S.)—Biography. 4. African American pioneers—West (U.S.)—Biography. 5. African American trappers—West (U.S.)—Biography. 6. African Americans—Biography. 7. Crow Indians.] I. Title.

F592 .B3975 D46 2007

978.02092—dc22   LCCN 2006932301

Printed by Star Standard Industries, Ltd., Singapore

Contents

2781

0

Why Write— or Read—a Book about Jim?

(Hey! Please read this Chapter 0 before charging on to Chapter 1.)

Jim Beckwourth was, in my opinion, a fantastic person, and most people who knew him agreed. They said Jim was smart, brave, kind, fun-loving, and friendly. They felt that he had good judgment and superior skills to those of other men who lived during his day. Few men have ever had more adventures involving life-threatening danger.

Jim was born a slave, was freed, and became a mountain man—one of the best of these tough characters. Mountain men were among the first explorers, other than the Indians, of the western wilderness of the American continent 200 years ago. Folks living during Jim's lifetime on the East Coast of the United States eagerly read about the lives of mountain men in

View of Beckwourth Valley (now called Sierra Valley), California, taken from the top of Beckwourth Peak. Jim's ranch was on the edge of this valley.

books and newspapers. These men became superheroes to the easterners, and Jim certainly enjoyed being a superhero.

Jim played a large part in helping Americans understand the geography of the great new West. The trails that mountain men like Jim pioneered became routes followed by emigrants (Americans moving to settle the West). These routes eventually became roads, and then superhighways. What pioneer men like Jim discovered and learned and taught others was enormously important in the settlement of the Wild West and the building of our great nation.

■ ■ ■

Before you read the story of this superhero, I first want to tell you how I got information about him.

How does anybody write a book about somebody who was born over 200 years ago? I couldn't ask people who knew him—they would have died over 100 years ago. To find out about the guy, I had to read what other people wrote about him long ago. Some of those people knew him, and others had merely talked to people who had known him. I also read more modern books written by historians who had done research about Jim.

Now, if a guy had written the story of his own life, that'd be the best source of information, wouldn't you think? Well, Jim did write a book about himself, called *The Life and Adventures of James P. Beckwourth*. So I read that, too.

Actually, Jim didn't write the book himself. During the long winter of 1854–1855, a newspaperman from Boston named Thomas Bonner listened while Jim told his life's story. Bonner supposedly wrote down just what Jim told him without changing what Jim had said. Did Jim agree to this because he couldn't write? Nope. Jim could read and write, but not with enough style to make a really good book. But he was a super storyteller, so telling the story of his life aloud was the way to go.

Now, if you think that Jim's book is all I'd need in order to learn about his life, you'd be wrong! You see, Jim exaggerated a lot in telling Bonner about his life. Sure, he did a lot of exciting things, but he made them sound even more exciting than they actually were. Some of the fantastic things that Jim said had happened to him most likely didn't actually happen at all or at least didn't happen in the way his book said. Bonner, too, did his own exaggerating. Jim might have been disappointed to see how Bonner had puffed up Jim's story in his book.

Well, was Jim just a big liar? Is his book useless because it has a bunch of inaccuracies? Heck no. Those who say that this or that story wasn't true weren't there themselves, so how do they know? Some later writers were able to prove that an Indian raid had only 200 Indians, not 2,000 as Jim said, but it still was a dangerous raid, and just because Jim's numbers are exaggerated doesn't make the story worthless.

Why did Jim exaggerate the stories he told Bonner? Well, mountain men told tall tales. The West had no buildings to stay in, so they camped out all the time, and of course there were no TVs, radios, computer games, iPods, or other forms of entertainment. Every evening after dinner, the men would sit around the campfire telling one another stories of adventures

An old log corral just around the corner from the site of a cabin where Jim had a trading post near the Middle Fork of the Feather River in California. That's Beckwourth Peak in the background.

they'd had. Now, all of them had adventures, so each story-teller would "puff up" his story to impress the others. Jim, being one of the very best ever to tell a story around the campfire, was so accustomed to exaggeration that he naturally did it with the stories he told to Bonner.

For another thing, Jim was 55 when he and Bonner teamed up, and it isn't possible for people that old to remember exactly how things happened many years before.

So, in the chapters that follow I'll sometimes refer to what Jim said in his book, especially when what he said sounds like it might have been the way it actually happened. But, as you read my story about Jim, if it seems to you that some stories may not have happened exactly that way, I say, so what? A bit of exaggeration doesn't make his book useless.

By the way, Bonner had agreed to pay Jim half the profits from the sale of *The Life and Adventures of James P. Beckwourth*. The book was a best seller, because, in the 1850s when it was published, folks in the eastern United States were fascinated by stories of what was happening in the wild, unpopulated region west of the Mississippi River. The book was reprinted in England and translated into French, so Jim became a hero in Europe, too. But Bonner cheated Jim and never paid him any of the large profits from the book.

So, here we go, following Jim's wild life from birth to death.

■ ■ ■

Special Note on Names of Groups

To be considerate of people's feelings today, I should use the words *African American*, *Native American*, and *Hispanic American*.

But during Jim's lifetime those words were unknown. Because this book is all about Jim's time (around 1800 to 1866), I've used the words used in that era. African Americans were called *Negroes* or *blacks*, Native Americans were called *Indians*, and Hispanic Americans were called *Mexicans*. I know that I'm not being correct by modern standards, but for proper historical flavor I've used the words from the years between 1800 and 1866. I hope you won't object.

■ ■ ■

Special Note on the Word Slave

Jim's own book never uses the word *slave* or *slavery*. Books written about Jim in later years use those words only to describe his status at birth and his eventual release from slavery by his father. During most of Jim's lifetime slavery was a fact of life of the United States. The Civil War (1861–1865) occurred toward the end of Jim's life. Lincoln's Emancipation Proclamation (1863), which declared slaves to be free, was issued three years before Jim died. What's more, it applied only to the southern states that had seceded from the Union. In the border states that stayed loyal to the United States, slavery was untouched by the proclamation. If Jim had remained a slave until 1863, this book would tell a very different story. Fortunately, his father, who owned him, gave Jim his freedom at an early age so that he was able to live his life of adventure, accomplishment, and independence.

1

Jim's Mom, Dad, and Granddad

Jim's father was the white owner of a cotton and tobacco plantation named Winders in Virginia. His mom was one of his father's black slaves on the plantation. So, Jim was bi-racial (both black and white), and, because his mother was a slave at the time he was born, he automatically became a slave.

We don't know anything about Jim's mother. It surprised me that Jim didn't even mention her in his book. There's no record showing that Jim's dad ever married her. When Jim's dad sold his plantation in Virginia and moved to St. Louis, he owned a bunch of slaves, and it has been assumed that she was one of them. We don't even know what her name was or if Jim's dad ever freed her from slavery. Jim had two bi-racial sisters whom his dad freed from slavery along with Jim. These sisters continued to live in St. Louis after they became adults.

Jim's book did mention his father in several places. His name was Jennings Beckwith. No, I didn't misspell his last name. The family name had always been spelled *Beckwith*, but

7

when Jim became an adult he decided that he preferred to spell it *Beckwourth.* No one knows why or exactly when he changed the spelling. In those days changing your name was easy—you just did it. Jim didn't have to change his name on his driver's license because cars hadn't been invented yet. Slaves didn't have birth certificates or legal papers of any sort to show they were citizens of the United States because, before the Civil War, they weren't considered citizens.

Jim's dad was called Sir Jennings by most people, because his great-great-grandfather had been knighted (declared to be a knight, a high-ranking nobleman) by the King of England. The Beckwiths were among the most famous knights in England. The "Sir" (which all men who are knighted use before their first name) was passed down from one generation to the next. However, Sir Jennings wasn't supposed to use the "Sir." After defeating the British in the Revolutionary War, the Americans set up the country without noblemen, so no American was supposed to use the British title "Sir" anymore.

Jim's dad had fought in the Revolutionary War. He was given the rank of captain when he was only 19, which was a mighty young age at which to command a hundred or so soldiers.

After the war, in 1787, Sir Jennings married Catherine Miskell, daughter of a prominent white Virginia family. They had three sons (Jim's half-brothers). Those three boys stayed in Virginia when the rest of the family moved west. Nobody knows what happened to Catherine or when she died. All we know is that in 1800 when Sir Jennings sold the plantation he'd inherited from his father, Catherine's name wasn't on any of the sale papers. According to Virginia law at the time, it should have been, so she probably had died before

*The main house on the Mount Airy Plantation near Warsaw, Virginia,
which is said to look much like the plantation house in which Jim's father
lived in Frederick County, Virginia, when Jim was born. The slaves'
quarters would have been behind the main house. Jim's dad died at Mount
Airy while visiting in 1835. (Courtesy of C. E. Miller and the Richmond
County Museum.)*

1800. It's possible that she and Sir Jennings were divorced,
but that's unlikely, because divorce was extremely rare in
those days.

The last year that Sir Jennings's name appears in the Virginia tax records is 1801, and 1809 is when his name appears
in Missouri records. Between those years, he seems to have
disappeared—his name doesn't come up anywhere in county
and state record books during those eight years. Jim's book
says that when he was eight or nine years old his father moved
with all his slaves to St. Louis.

No one knows why Jennings Beckwith (he dropped the "Sir" when he got to St. Louis) made the move, because it was very unusual for a family to sell a fine Virginia plantation and move to a tiny frontier town way "out west" in Missouri. If you look at a modern map of the United States, Missouri is right in the middle of the country, not "way out west," isn't it? However, in the early 1800s almost nothing was known about the land west of Missouri, so St. Louis was as far west as anybody knew.

Jennings might have moved because the Beckwith family had both black and white members, and many white Virginians didn't approve of bi-racial families. The small pioneer

The mill pond near the Mount Airy plantation. Jim's grandfather's plantation, not far from here, also had a mill and mill pond. The mill, built at the outlet of the dammed pond, had a waterwheel that turned the grinding stones. Wheat was ground into flour for making bread and cakes.

town of St. Louis was inhabited by a mix of French, Spanish, Canadian, and American folks, so having a bi-racial family would certainly have been more acceptable there.

St. Louis really was a small town then, with only 1,100 residents. Today St. Louis County has a population of more than a million, so it has grown a bit in the past 200 years. Evidently, even in the 1800s the town was too big for Jim's dad, so he moved his family out of town into the wilderness (you'll read about the Beckwith place called The Point in Chapter 2). I think that Jim inherited from his dad some of his desire to wander from one place to another.

Although Jim's book doesn't mention his grandfather (his dad's dad), I found out quite a bit about him. His name was Jonathan Beckwith, and, like Jim's father, he used his knight's title, so people called him Sir Jonathan. He was well known in the part of Virginia in which he lived and became fairly wealthy. Upon his death, he owned 34 slaves. In those days some folks judged how rich a person was by how many slaves he or she owned. Yes, women owned slaves, too. Catherine Miskell, Sir Jennings's wife, inherited some from her father, and George Washington's wife, Martha, owned quite a few—as did George himself. What a lousy way to decide how rich somebody was!

Sir Jonathan was a difficult person who evidently quarreled with everyone he knew, especially his own family. He wanted to do everything his own way. Someone once said that Sir Jonathan preferred the company of his dogs to the company of his neighbors. Maybe Jim inherited from his granddad his desire to be different from everybody else.

Naturally, if we don't know about Jim's mother, we don't know anything about her father or mother. I wonder if Jim ever wished he knew more about his family.

The beautiful St. Louis arch on the Mississippi Riverfront. Jim would have landed at this site many years before the arch was built, when his family moved to St. Louis.

We do know that, after his kids were all grown, Jim's dad eventually moved back to Virginia. The family fortune was long gone. When Jim's father died, at the age of 72, he might even have been considered homeless and poor, a sad ending for someone who had once been a leading citizen of Virginia. Jim was living with the Crow Indians at that time and received no word about his father's death. Not until several years later, when he visited St. Louis for the first time in almost 14 years, did he learn that his dad had died in Virginia.

2

Jim the Kid, Teenager, and Young Man

Jim was born on April 26, 1798—maybe. How come maybe? Well, in the first sentence of Jim's book he says that he was born on that date, and you'd think a man would know his own birthday, wouldn't you? However, many people, for one reason or another, don't tell other people their correct birth date. (For example, many years ago some kids—who, me?—lied about their birth dates to get driver's licenses when they were only 15. Of course, that doesn't work nowadays.) Maybe Jim didn't know his birth date because many slaves were never told when they were born, and no records were kept of their birth dates. As slaves became adults, they might have to guess what their birth date might be.

Historians who have done research about Jim's life discovered that the year 1800 for his birth fits much better with other known facts. I vote for 1800 instead of 1798, so that's the date I'll use throughout this book.

What was going on in 1800? George Washington had died the year before, and John Adams was busy being the young country's second president. The famous Lewis and Clark Expedition hadn't yet begun. Although a few Spanish explorers had traveled from Mexico into the far west of the continent, very few Americans had traveled west of the Mississippi River.

Only Indians knew of the land that now is Missouri, Kansas, Nebraska, Montana, Idaho, and Colorado. The Wild West was still mighty wild. The United States was a tiny young nation with only 16 states.

What do we know about Jim's life on the Virginia plantation before the age of eight? Not much. In his book he describes hearing his father's friends discussing over and over their part in the Revolutionary War. That's about it. Jim admits that his memory of his childhood was mostly wiped out by all the adventures he had after the age of eight.

When Jim was about eight years old (the exact date is unknown) his dad moved his whole family to St. Louis. We know that by September 1809 Jennings Beckwith had moved to St. Charles, just north of St. Louis, and in August 1810 he bought 1,280 acres called The Point near St. Charles. The Point is where the Mississippi River and the Missouri River join. The area was nothing but wilderness, covered with trees and bushes that had to be removed to make part of the land suitable for farming. It also wasn't easy to get from The Point to St. Louis, because, although the distance was only 15 miles, there were no good roads, and the wide Missouri River blocked the way. A bridge across the river wasn't built until many years later, so to go to town the Beckwiths had to take a boat across the river.

When Jim lived at The Point, the region had unfriendly Indians and few neighbors. According to Jim's book, one day

Site of The Point where Jim's dad moved the family from St. Louis. The Missouri River on the left joins the darker-colored Mississippi River on the right. That road leading to the point of land wasn't there in Jim's day. He lived in St. Louis while he was going to school, but spent his summers at The Point when school was out.

while he was on an errand, he stopped at a neighboring farm to say hello to some friends. Jim was shocked to discover that his friend, all of his friend's sisters and brothers, and their parents had been killed and scalped by Indians. I hope you don't ever see a scalped person, because it's pretty gross. The skin and hair on the top of a scalped person's head are cut off and kept by the scalper as a trophy of what he (I've never heard of a she scalper) did. The more scalps an Indian warrior had, the more popular he became within his tribe. Jim's book points out that his father got a bunch of his buddies together and they tracked down the Indians who had committed these murders. All the Indians were killed—and scalped, to show that white men could do scalping too. Wow, am I glad that awful practice stopped over 100 years ago!

In those days, slaves rarely went to school. But Jim's dad, who obviously loved him, wanted him to have some education and sent Jim to attend school in St. Louis. It took far too long to travel every day from The Point to St. Louis, so Jim lived in town away from his family during the school year. It was during this time that his dad decided to free Jim from slavery. On three separate occasions, Mr. Beckwith went to court to make Jim's freedom official.

Jim attended school for only three or four years, but that was as long as many kids went in those days. He learned to

View of the rivers joining at The Point. In this photo the Missouri is on the right and the Mississippi on the left. That's me enjoying the view.

read, write, and do basic math, making him better educated than a large part of the people living in the United States in the early 1800s.

I couldn't find much information about Jim's teenage years. I do know that he worked as a blacksmith for a man named George Casner for about three years, until he was 19 years old.

Jim's book describes the end of his blacksmith career. One day, Casner criticized him for not working hard. In his book, Jim admits to goofing off a bit because his thoughts were on a young lady whom he had been dating (I'm not sure they called it dating in 1819). Jim didn't like being criticized by his boss, so they got into a fight, which Jim won. Beating up your boss isn't a good thing to do if you want to keep a job. Casner fired Jim on the spot.

In writing this chapter I wondered whether I should tell you about this fight, because it doesn't make Jim sound like the good guy he became. However, many successful people have a less-than-perfect beginning, so I decided to leave it in. Jim evidently learned his lesson, because historians who have researched Jim's life don't mention any other times he got in trouble with people he worked for (well, except for one time, when he was accused of borrowing some horses and never returning them).

To avoid more trouble, Jim decided to leave St. Louis. He had met some men who planned to travel up the Mississippi River by boat for 20 days to a place called Fever River (it's now Galena, Illinois). There they hoped to make a treaty with the Sac Indian tribe so that the group could open a lead mine. In those days lead was used for plumbing pipes, before anyone figured out that people died from consuming small amounts of this metal. Jim's dad hoped Jim would

Jim worked in a blacksmith shop in St. Louis much like this one when he was a teenager. This blacksmith shop is near the old ghost town of Eureka Mills, about a half-hour drive from Jim's California ranch in the Sierra mountains.

return to blacksmithing, but Jim wanted no part of it. So he was allowed to join the group heading for Fever River.

This was when Jim's life of adventure began. He worked only part-time in the lead mine, and during his free time he became friendly with some of the Indian men about his age.

They taught Jim how to hunt, shoot a bow and arrow, and master other Indian skills. For the remainder of his life, this part of Jim's "education" was very useful to him, especially when he became an early mountain man in the Wild West. After 18 months, Jim returned to St. Louis, where the trouble he'd had with his old boss had "blown over" and been forgotten. But Jim now knew that a life of adventure was what he wanted.

He was offered a job as a keeper of horses by General William Ashley, who was leading a group of men westward into the wilderness, where few men other than Indians had ever been before. The rest of Jim's education came from these mountain men. They taught him the skills he needed to live independently far from civilization in the wilderness.

Jim learned quickly. In later years his ability to learn other languages was a great help in dealing with people of many tribes and nationalities. Besides English, he could speak and understand French, Spanish, and four Indian languages. Even with only four years of schooling, his experiences made him one of the best-educated men in the Old West. Education can be many kinds of learning besides reading and writing English and knowing how to add, subtract, multiply, and divide.

There is another part of Jim's education that he didn't learn at school in St. Louis. Back in Virginia, in the 1800s, plantation owners like his father, were expected to have refined manners. Jim's dad taught Jim how to act with courtesy and be nice to everyone. So Jim was able to fit in with all kinds of people from all levels of society. Many people he met expected him to be a rude, crude, rough, gruff fellow—they were happily surprised at his excellent manners.

3

Jim Becomes a Mountain Man

Who were the mountain men? They were just about the bravest, roughest, toughest, most independent bunch that ever lived in North America. About 200 years ago there were a small number, maybe only 250 or 300, who ventured into the wilderness.

These rugged men journeyed into the Wild West where only Indians had been before. They traveled on foot and on horseback. They had no maps or trails to tell them how to get to where they wanted to go. Actually, most of the time they didn't even *know* where they wanted to go. All they knew was that they needed to get to the western plains and the Rocky Mountains so that they could trap beavers (Chapter 5 will tell you why they wanted beaver skins).

It took them three or four months to travel from St. Louis or other new towns along the Mississippi River to the creeks in the Wild West where the beavers lived. It's amazing to think that today you can travel this same distance in about two hours in a jet airplane.

They traveled through plenty of places where unfriendly Indians lived, and many mountain men were killed by them. Others died from a variety of causes—bear wounds, disease, starvation, drowning, accidents causing major injury, or freezing. Those mountain men who escaped these dangers and lived for many years in the wilderness learned to stay alive by being smarter or by staying in better physical condition.

They learned by experience, because there were no books, magazines, classroom teachers, or Internet sites to teach them how to stay alive. They also learned from one another.

Living such a rough and tough life, they became good at hunting, good at pathfinding, good at fixing their own equipment, good at sleeping on the ground every night with no air mattress, pillow, or warm sleeping bag, good at doing first aid, good at avoiding danger, and good at getting along with their fellow mountain men.

During the winter, they traveled through snow in the

This is how Jim would have looked as a mountain man. (Statuette courtesy of Laura Root from the series "All God's Children," Martha Originals, Inc.)

Ruins of the hospital at Fort Laramie in Wyoming. During his traveling
years as a mountain man Jim stopped at Fort Laramie several times.

mountains with only a couple of blankets and almost never a
tent. In the heat of summer, they traveled with no air condi-
tioning, no sunblock, no cold sodas or popsicles. They didn't
have bug lotion, so mosquitoes, flies, and biting insects feasted
on them.

None of them got rich by trapping. Mostly they worked for
different fur companies who supplied their equipment but
paid them poorly. Salaries were between $200 and $400 per
year! Eventually most mountain men became "free trappers,"
working for themselves. Even though this let them roam where
they wanted rather than where their boss said to go, they still
were poor.

Jim's first experience in becoming a mountain man was
when he was 24. He was asked by General William Ashley to travel with 25 other men to the Rocky Mountains to

trap beavers. Jim had already learned a lot about Indians by becoming friends with them a year before, when he was part of a group of men who had gone to Fever River. His experience as a blacksmith was also useful because he knew how to shoe horses. Jim did such a good job for General Ashley that he became one of the general's most trusted and appreciated trappers.

Mountain men seldom washed their clothes, seldom changed their underwear, seldom had a bath—other than a dip in a cold lake or stream now and then. They didn't shampoo their hair or brush their teeth. Can you imagine how these guys smelled? Whew! What did they care? They were used to each other, stink and all.

Many mountain men had never been to school so they couldn't read or write. Jim, who could read well and write adequately was the exception. But out in the wilderness there were no books, magazines, or newspapers, so it didn't matter if a man couldn't read. There was no mail and no need for writing.

As the Wild West became less wild, and settlers started to move to the area, the few remaining mountain men disappeared. Well, actually they didn't "disappear," they merely found other jobs and

Bronze sculpture of a mountain man by the artist, Frederic Remington, who was famous for sculptures and paintings of the old West. (Sculpture from the author's private collection.)

returned to a more civilized life. That must have been difficult, because they were used to being independent, without the rules and regulations of civilization.

Jim became one of the all-time best mountain men and lasted longer living in the wilderness than most of his companions. He escaped death many times (read about some of his near-death experiences in Chapter 9). Finally, he, too, left the wilderness. But he hadn't saved up any money, so he had to find jobs. He didn't like doing any one thing for very long— he'd get bored, and he'd itch to see new places and meet new people, so he'd quit and seek out something else to do. You'll enjoy reading about all the different jobs he did in Chapter 16. He definitely was accepted back into civilization, so I'm sure that he bathed more often and wore cleaner clothes—he knew how to clean up his act.

4

A Joke Makes Jim a Crow Indian

One summer, Jim and several other mountain men began living with a small group of Crow Indians. The Crows called Jim White-Handled Knife.

Some of the mountain men fought, along with Crow men, against warriors from the neighboring Blackfoot tribe and won the battle. Jim evidently was one of the fiercest fighters. When the group returned to the main village of the Crows, they were asked about the victory, and they related that White-Handled Knife was the bravest of all. The village was very impressed that someone who was not an Indian had done so well.

One of the mountain men living among the Crows was a guy by the name of Caleb Greenwood, who was married to a Crow woman and spoke the Crow language. As a joke, Caleb told the members of the village that Jim was actually a Crow Indian. He said that Jim had been stolen from the Crows when he was a baby by some Cheyenne Indians, and he'd stayed with them

Most tepees, called "lodges" by the Indians, were covered with buffalo hides. During the years when Jim lived with the Crows, he would have lived in a tepee that looked like this one. (Courtesy of the Buffalo Bill Historical Center, Cody, WY.)

ever since. Jim went along with the gag and didn't tell the Crows that Caleb was merely joking.

Several weeks later, Jim went beaver trapping with one of his good buddies, Jim Bridger, who was another of the Wild West's most famous mountain men. The two Jims parted company, each taking a different branch of the stream on which they were trapping. "Our" Jim suddenly discovered that he was surrounded by unfriendly Crow Indians. He surrendered his gun and traps, but luckily, instead of killing him on the spot, the Indians took him back to their village. Someone in the Crow village remembered Caleb's story that this captured man was a good fighter and had been born a Crow but had been stolen by the Cheyennes. This news caused a great commotion in the village as all the old women rushed to see if Jim might be their long-lost son. The women examined him from head to foot, looking for a mark on his body that would enable one of them to claim White-Handled Knife as her own boy.

The thorough examination produced no defining mark until one old woman said, "If this is my son, he has a mole over one of his eyes."

Jim's eyelids were pulled down, and, sure enough, she discovered a mole just over his left eye. The woman was the wife of Big Bowl, who then was declared Jim's father by the group.

Jim's book relates, "They seized me in their arms and hugged me. My face positively burned with the enraptured kisses of my numerous fair sisters, with a long host of cousins, aunts, and more other remote kindred."

Big Bowl excitedly told the village, "The dead is alive again and the lost one is found." He knew this was true because Caleb had said so, and the Crows didn't believe that the white man would tell a lie.

Jim's four new "sisters" dressed him in the best Crow clothing so that he looked like one of the most popular warriors in the tribe. That evening, Big Bowl asked Jim if he'd like a Crow wife. Although Jim couldn't yet speak much of the Crow language, he indicated to his new "father" that he'd appreciate having a tribal wife. Three beautiful sisters, daughters of one of the tribe's favorite warriors, were presented to Jim from which to pick his bride. He chose Still Water, the oldest of the three. A joyous marriage ceremony in the best Crow tradition was held the next day.

Jim enjoyed his new life as a Crow, so he didn't tell any of the tribe that it was all a joke. Caleb must have had a good laugh to learn that his joke had made Jim a member of the Crow tribe. As the years passed, tribal members finally realized that Jim hadn't been born a Crow and that they'd been fooled. However, Jim fit in so well with the tribe and was so highly respected and liked that they didn't care if it had all started as a joke.

I've asked myself how a black man could be thought to be an Indian. One of the books I read about Jim's life answered my question this way: "There are many shades of men even among the many Indian tribes." Indeed, throughout Jim's years living with the Crows, other tribes didn't question whether Jim was actually a Crow

Buffalo hide being stretched on a frame to dry and cure. When dried they made a good covering for the outside of a tepee or rug for the tepee floor. (Courtesy of the Buffalo Bill Historical Center, Cody, WY.)

or not. When Jim dressed as an Indian, wore his hair long in Indian fashion, and painted his face before going into battle or for celebrations, he certainly must have been unrecognizable as a black man.

It also seemed unusual to me that Caleb, a white man, would live with the Crows and marry one. But history books tell us that the Crows were kind to white men who came to live among them. Evidently it was not so strange for a white man to take a Crow wife. Extremely few white or black women traveled to the old West in those days. So, when mountain men wanted female companionship, they turned to friendly tribes such as the Crows, who didn't seem to mind having their women marry mountain men.

Of those trappers and white travelers who wanted to experience the life of an Indian, few stayed for as many years as Jim did. In his book, he tells about his first Christmas as a Crow. Of course the Indians knew nothing about the birth of Christ or Christianity so Jim celebrated Christmas by himself. He decided that it was too difficult to explain Christianity to the tribe, so he didn't even try to tell them what Christmas was all about. Although Jim was well loved by the tribe, he must have had some lonely times among them, too.

5

Jim Becomes Chief and Helps the Crows in War and Trade

The Crow nation had six counselors (kind of like sub-chiefs). Together with the head chief, they ruled the tribe. The office of first counselor had equal authority with the head chief. The sixth counselor was the lowest in influence. This was like the U.S. army, where a soldier who is made an officer starts at the lowest rank (second lieutenant) and after years of advancing into higher ranks might eventually become a general. First, a Crow man (there were no women sub-chiefs or head chiefs) had to start as a common warrior. As his accomplishments grew, he'd work his way up into the counselor ranks.

Naturally, when Jim first joined the tribe he started at the bottom. During his first years he learned the Crows' language and customs. You probably already know Jim well enough to guess that he wouldn't be satisfied merely staying at the

30

bottom. As his expertise in warfare grew, so did his influence and popularity among the Crows. He gained the Indians' trust and became the Crows' sixth counselor. At that point they were calling him Bloody Arm.

By the time Jim began to move up through the counselor ranks, many of the tribal members had realized that he wasn't a kidnapped Crow son (see the story in Chapter 4) and wasn't an Indian at all but had just been adopted as a Crow. Still, Jim was so thoroughly trusted and admired by the Crows and had become so completely like a Crow that they didn't care if he wasn't an Indian by birth.

Eventually, Jim became the second-most-powerful Crow after only Long Hair, whom the Indians called A-ra-poo-ash. When Long Hair was mortally wounded by a bunch of Black-foot warriors, he told the Crow braves who were with him at the scene of the battle that Bloody Arm (Jim) should become the head chief.

So, there Jim was, the most powerful person in the Crow nation. But was he? Like so many other parts of the story of Jim's life (especially those described in his book) this tale raised questions: had Jim actually become the number one Crow? A couple of white men who had also lived with the Crows wrote that Jim wasn't the head chief. Still, maybe these guys were jealous that Jim became so popular with the Crows when they themselves didn't, so they purposely tried to make Jim sound less successful than he actually was. I guess we'll never know for sure. Here's something to think about, though: many years later, when Jim was testifying under oath in a court of law on behalf of the U.S. government, he was asked if he had been chief of the Crows. He said, "Yes," and most historians believe that Jim, in this instance, was telling the truth.

A more modern tepee—it has a decorated canvas covering outside instead of buffalo hide.

Why was Jim so popular with the Crows? Was it just because he was a good fighter? Nope. It was because he made the Crows the most successful of all the tribes in the plains and Rocky Mountains.

One of his best accomplishments was changing how the Crows fought battles against the other tribes. All the tribes used the same method of attack. They would make a mad dash at their opponents, perhaps killing a few, and then immediately retreat, losing all the power of their first aggressive attack. Jim showed them that this method of fighting could be improved. He had the chance to be part of a Crow war party that attacked eleven members of the Blood tribe. When the Crows retreated from their first rapid charge, Jim didn't—he continued fighting. As the Crows withdrew, they noticed with surprise that Jim had stayed behind and was fighting the battle alone, one man against eleven. The Crows turned around and rushed back to help him. The Bloods, who were used to having their opponents retreat after a first thrust, were caught completely off guard, and the Crows won a decisive victory. By this example Jim changed his tribe's fighting tactic to one that made them very successful in battle.

Another great contribution Jim made to his tribe was introducing a fairer way of trading with the white men at the trading posts (which actually were forts). The Indians would bring in cured buffalo robes and other animal skins to trade with the white men who ran the posts. The white traders carried the skins back to St. Louis, where they could be sold at a great profit. Because the Indians didn't know any better, they would receive cheap beads and worthless stuff in exchange for the valuable buffalo hides.

Unlike Jim, none of the Crows could speak good English, so they had a hard time trying to bargain for better trades. When Jim observed how his tribe was getting cheated by the white traders, he told his Crow friends, "Let me do all the trading for the whole tribe. I'll get you better things in exchange for your buffalo robes." So Jim told the traders that he wanted

Sketch of Jim dressed in his Crow Indian clothing, drawn by artist Maynard Dixon (1875–1946). Dixon was famous for painting scenes of the American West. This sketch was made in 1941 as an illustration for a limited edition reprint of Francis Parkman's book Oregon Trail. *(From a private collection, courtesy of Dr. Mark Sublette, Medicine Man Gallery, Santa Fe, NM.)*

guns, bullets, knives, axes, tools, and cooking pots in trade instead of some crummy jewelry.

But the traders said, "Forget it. We're not going to give guns to Indians. They might use them against us. Let them stick to their bows and arrows, which do us much less harm." I can't blame the traders for this, can you?

Then Jim "guaranteed" to the white traders that the Crows wouldn't use the guns or any other weapons against all white men. Because of Jim's good reputation among the traders of the plains and Rocky Mountains, they believed his "guarantee."

That was how Jim was able to get rifles and ammunition in exchange for buffalo robes.

Well, the result was that the Crows had rifles with which to fight other tribes who had only spears and bows and arrows. A rifle bullet goes much farther than an arrow and can be shot with a lot better accuracy. This far superior weaponry allowed the Crows to win most of their battles, and soon they were the most feared tribe among all their neighbors.

Jim made good on his "guarantee," and the Crows didn't attack the forts and trading posts or the white emigrants traveling through the Indians' territory. I suppose the pledge Jim made to the traders eventually was broken, but the history books speak in awe about the friendship of the Crows with all people except other Indians.

To increase the goods the Crows had available to trade, Jim taught them how to trap beavers. The traders prized beaver skins because they could be sold at good prices in St. Louis. Beaver hats were popular at that time in the eastern United States. Eventually beaver hats went out of fashion, fortunately for the beavers, who were rapidly being trapped out of existence.

Jim had to convince the Crows that trapping animals to get skins to trade was better than going off to fight neighboring tribes. Even though Jim's influence with his tribe was great, the braves eventually got tired of trapping and returned to the job they preferred—fighting. Then the number of beaver pelts that Jim could take to the trading post for the tribe decreased rapidly.

While he was chief, Jim also worked for one of the fur trading companies. When the tribe stopped trapping, the company became discouraged with Jim, because he no longer brought them as many beaver skins. However, if Jim had insisted that the Crows trap instead of going to battle, he would have lost his popularity within the tribe.

One other benefit Chief Jim brought to the Crows was the ability to recognize the value of peace with a neighboring tribe. True, the Blackfeet's dislike for the Crows ruled them out as a peaceful neighbor, but there were other, less warlike tribes that could become friendly neighbors. Indeed, the Snake tribe became well-liked by the Crows. They could peacefully visit one another's villages—the women would chat together, the kids play together, and the old men tell stories to one another. Trading between tribes was better for everyone.

You know, it seems to me that all nations today could learn a lesson from how Jim achieved peace between tribes and how peace was much better for everyone than war. Can you imagine how awesome it would be if Jim's idea became true throughout the world today?

There was one last thing that Jim required the Crows to do (or actually not do) that helped make them more success-ful than other tribal nations. While he was chief, Jim made a rule within the tribe that no Crows would drink whiskey. The braves of other tribes would often get wildly drunk. Eventu-ally, when they drank too much too often the men could no longer be useful members of the tribe. Then the whole tribal structure would fall apart, and the men couldn't hunt and fight properly. Jim didn't allow anyone in the Crow tribe to break his no-drinking rule. As a result the Crows stayed strong while their neighbors lost strength. Hooray for Jim!

6

A Man of Many Names

Although Jim's dad, granddad, and relatives before them spelled their last name Beckwith (see Chapter 1), Jim signed his name James P. Beckwourth. He called himself Jim, and all his buddies called him that, too.

The Indians didn't call him Jim, though. Before he joined the Crows, the Indians he knew called him a name that translated into English as White-Handled Knife. Nowhere have I been able to find out how the Indians chose this name for Jim, but maybe it was simply because he carried a knife with a white handle. Later, when the Crows thought he was a long-lost son and accepted him into the tribe (see Chapter 4), they named him Morning Sun.

The tradition among the Crows was that, after each deed of bravery, a man would be called by a different name. So, when Jim distinguished himself as a great warrior on his first outing, in a battle against a neighboring tribe, he was given the name Antelope.

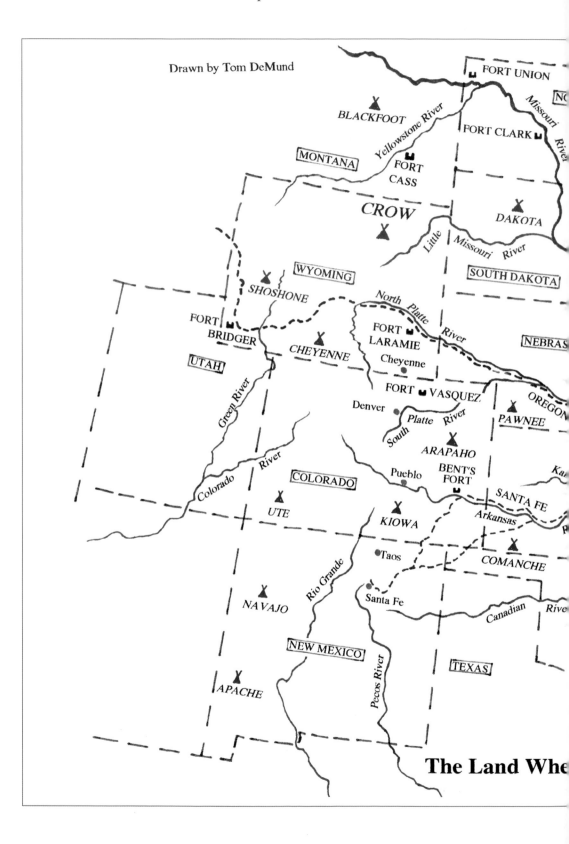

Drawn by Tom DeMund

The Land Whe

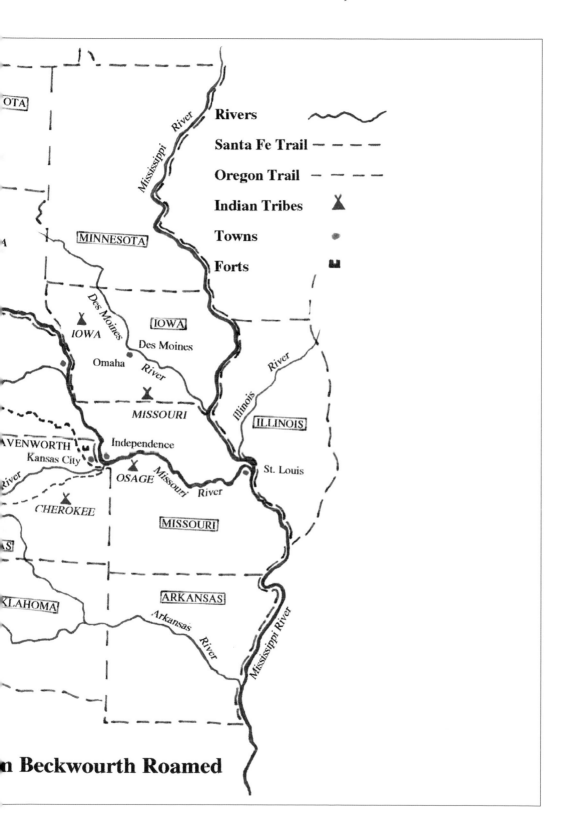

Rivers

Santa Fe Trail

Oregon Trail

Indian Tribes

Towns

Forts

Beckwourth Roamed

Almost every time Jim went out with the Crows to battle against other tribes, he was the most outstanding fighter (at least according to his book). Upon returning to the Crow village afterward he was given a new name. The name Big Bowl (Bat-te-Sarsh, in the Crow language) came next. Soon after, he led a raid on a Blackfoot tribal village by a group of Crow braves most of whom were his "brothers." When he and his brothers returned in triumph with a herd of 118 horses they had stolen from the Blackfeet, there was great joy among the Crows, and they then named Jim Enemy of Horses (Is-ko-chu-e-chu-re), since he had stolen so many. (It's funny that the Blackfeet didn't have black feet—but Jim did!)

The man who makes the first strike on an opposing Indian in battle is considered a great hero. In the next fight, Jim again struck down the first enemy—in this instance, a great chief. When the Crow war party returned with news of their victory, Jim was given the name Bull's Robe for slaying of the opposing chief.

Another battle in which Jim was the hero earned him the name Bobtail Horse (Shas-ka-ohush-a). After another victory he became known as Red Fish. On a following occasion he was given the name Bloody Arm (sometimes translated as Red Arm). That time, he, all by himself, charged an opposing group of Indians who were about to kill an old man. Jim drove them off for a few minutes, enough time for him to carry the old man back to safety. His bravery saved the life of his old friend and his own life.

He was known as Bloody Arm when, in a battle with the Blackfeet, the Crows' number one chief, A-ra-poo-ash, was mortally wounded. As the chief was dying, he called the Crow warriors together, saying that Bloody Arm was to become the number one chief. Jim was then given the name Good War Road.

Sometime later he received his final name, Medicine Calf (Nan-kup-bah-pah). The Crows believed that if a man was successful in battle and all other things, he had good "medicine," and that's how Jim came to be called by this final Crow name.

As the head chief, replacing A-ra-poo-ash, Jim had risen to the top of his fame. There was no way he could be given any greater honors by the tribe. For the remainder of his life, even after he left the Crows to have other adventures, the tribe remembered him as their Medicine Calf, their all-time great leader.

Some of the other tribes used the names chosen by the Crows. On one occasion many years after he'd left the Crows, Jim met some members of the Cheyenne tribe whom he had not seen for more than 20 years. He was instantly recognized and his presence was signaled for many miles to scattered members of the tribe. The Cheyennes came rushing from long distances to meet and welcome Jim, whom they fondly called Big Medicine, considering him greater than all the white men of the plains.

Count 'em: he had 11 different names during the years he lived with the Crows. But often in those years he'd visit with white men—either on trading trips to their forts or posts or when white trappers visited the Crow villages. The white men always called him Jim. They paid no attention to the names the Indians had given him.

I guess I'd rather be called Jim than Bloody Arm—how about you?

7

Chief Jim Leaves the Crows

Although Jim had successfully risen to the position of top chief of the Crows and had long been loved and appreciated by the tribe, he wasn't satisfied. True, the tribe had prospered under his leadership. Yet, he kept thinking that he had been wasting his life. As he said in his book, "What had I done? When I abandoned myself seriously to reflection, it seems as if I had slumbered away the last 12 years. Others had accomplished the same toils as myself and were now living in luxury and ease."

Although he had wives and a son among the Crows, part of Jim's sadness was that he hadn't seen his father's family in many years. He wondered if his dad was still alive and what had happened to his brothers and sisters.

He'd also heard from visiting trappers about wonderful things that were happening beyond the prairies where the Crows lived, things such as railroad trains that could be pulled all day long by a steam engine that never got tired. A whole new world had been born during the years Jim was living with the Crows, and he longed to see it.

Jim had originally left St. Louis to satisfy a youthful longing for adventure and independence. He'd joined the Crows for adventure and the excitement of battles with other tribes. He'd escaped death numerous times, and it was a miracle that he was still alive after so many close calls. He'd been wounded lots of times, too, and, even though he was only 43 years old, he knew that his super energy and good health couldn't last forever. Someday he'd be too old to travel and see the world beyond Crow territory. And, by now, Jim had tired of all the savagery, fighting, and killing.

So, he gathered the other Crow leaders and told them that he was leaving. His book describes his speech to them:

> Sparrow-Hawks [Crow was the name the white men gave the tribe, but the Indians called themselves Sparrow-Hawks], I am going to leave you for a few moons [a few months] to visit my friends among the white men. I shall return to you by green grass [spring] when the boats come back from the country of the whites. While I am away, I desire you to remember the counsel I have often given you. I want you to send out no war parties because you want for nothing and your nation is feared by all the neighboring tribes . . . . Do not let the Blackfeet or any other bad Indians harm them [the white men at the neighboring fort where the Crows traded]. Behave yourselves.

We can't be sure if Jim actually planned to return when the grass turned green or whether his promise was merely a way of making the Crows feel better about having their great chief leave them.

Jim traveled by boat downstream on the Yellowstone River, stopping for three days at Fort Union. There he had a canoe built for him. The trip he then made to St. Louis took several weeks.

At one camping place along the river Jim shot and cooked a couple of fat wild turkeys. He'd been eating only buffalo meat for many years, because there were no wild turkeys in the Crows' territory. The juicy turkey dinner was one of the best meals he'd had in years.

Several days before arriving at St. Louis, Jim got a high fever. He was so eager to get home that he refused to go ashore at the next town, Jefferson City, to rest up and get well. Instead, he put the canoe on a passing paddle-wheel boat and continued down the Missouri River to St. Louis. When he arrived at the dock, he was too sick to take much notice of anything and immediately rushed to where his family had lived. His sister Louise answered his knock on the door, but she didn't recognize him—he was dressed in the strange clothes worn by mountain men, and his long hair reached almost to his waist, which was how the Crows liked to wear their hair.

"Don't you recognize your own brother?" Jim asked.

Then Louise was overjoyed, because word had reached St. Louis that Jim had been killed in a battle with the Blackfoot tribe. Louise called to Jim's oldest sister, Matilda, who came downstairs and was also thrilled to find her wandering brother alive.

Jim was so sick that he couldn't really celebrate with his sisters. After asking a few questions, he went right to bed.

The Big Horn River where it flows through the Crow Indian Reservation in Montana. Jim probably floated downstream in a small boat past this spot when he left the Crows.

Unfortunately, the answers to his questions were not what he'd hoped to hear. His father had moved back to Virginia many years ago and had died there. His brothers had left St. Louis and lived elsewhere. Eliza, the girl Jim had fallen in love with when he'd lived in St. Louis as a young man, had married another man.

Several days later Jim was well enough to head out to explore the new St. Louis and visit his old friends. Most of his friends had moved or died. The ones he did find seemed changed from their younger days. When he'd finished walking around town, he realized that this wasn't the same small community he fondly remembered. The little village of muddy streets he'd left 12 years before had become a busy center of trade. There wasn't much in St. Louis that appealed to him now.

He thought of his Indian friends and how greatly honored he'd been to become a chief of the Crows. He had acquired Indian habits and had helped to improve the tribe. He thought of his son and Crow wives. He became restless and thought about returning to the tribe.

One day his decision to return to the Crows was made for him. A messenger arrived in St. Louis with an urgent request for Jim to return to Fort Cass. The Crows had been told that their favorite chief, Medicine Calf (Jim, of course), had been killed by the whites while on his visit to St. Louis. They advanced on Fort Cass and planned to retaliate by killing all the white people at the fort. The fort wasn't well enough protected or strong enough to hold off an assault by the Crows, but luckily a man named Tullock, who ran the trading post at the fort, was a good friend of the Crows. He pleaded with the Indians not to kill all the whites—including himself! Tullock promised that Medicine Calf would return by the time the cherries on the cherry trees turned red—although, he didn't know for sure himself whether Jim was alive or dead. The Crows agreed to put off the massacre of the fort's occupants to see if their favorite chief would return by the appointed time. If he didn't, the fort's white people were goners.

Jim had to leave St. Louis immediately, because the a trip to Fort Cass was 2,000 miles. There were no wagon roads, so Jim had to travel on horseback through wilderness full of dangerous Indians who weren't friends of the Crows. Traveling westward couldn't be done by canoe or other boat on the rivers, because the rivers all flowed easterly, and no paddled or rowed boat could make much westward progress against the current.

The fastest trip to Fort Cass might take 53 days, so off Jim rushed to beat the ripening of the cherries. After several dangerous adventures along the way, he arrived at Fort Cass just in time. He gave the Crows a good scolding for believing that their Medicine Calf had been killed.

However, Jim's short return to St. Louis hadn't convinced him to remain with the Crows for the rest of his life. The reasons he'd left were still in his thoughts. So, once again, he told the tribe that he was leaving and didn't tell them that he wouldn't return.

As the years passed without his return, the Crows finally accepted the fact that their heroic chief had left them forever. And he actually did return to them once again, but you'll have to keep reading this book to discover what happened then.

8

Jim, the Athlete

Jim must have been a very athletic guy, although I can't say he was an athlete. How come? Well, to be an athlete, a person needs to take part in athletics—games or sports requiring physical skill. In the 1800s when Jim lived, baseball, football, basketball, and other sports had not yet been "invented." There weren't colleges or even high schools as we know them today; there were no professional sports. However, there were sporting events, so let me tell you about them, and maybe you'll decide that we should call Jim an athlete after all.

In 1825 when Jim was on his third year-long trip to the Rocky Mountains for trapping beavers, his boss, General Ashley, founded what was then called the "Rendezvous" (a French word, pronounced ron-day-voo, meaning "meeting"). Some people called it the "Mountain Fair." You see, before that year, by midsummer, after the mountain men had finished their trapping activities, they'd carry their beaver skins back to St. Louis to sell and buy supplies for the next twelve months. Then they'd carry the supplies back to the Rocky Mountains. The trips to St. Louis and back would take about five months.

Site of the 1829 Rendezvous where Jim might have participated in various athletic activities. This site is near today's town of Landers, Wyoming, on the Popo Agie River.

General Ashley had a brilliant idea: Wouldn't it be easier and cheaper to bring a bunch of wagons loaded with all the needed supplies from St. Louis to the mountains, when the trapping season ended in July, and have all the scattered trappers meet the wagons at once? They could trade their beaver skins for the supplies they needed without each trapper having to make the long trek to St. Louis.

Well, when all these rough and rowdy mountain men were gathered at one place you can imagine what happened next—party time! The first Rendezvous in 1825 lasted only one extra day and it was "dry" (without booze), because the general didn't approve of drinking. However, later Rendezvous (there were 16 in all, scattered at different places throughout the mountains) were "wet." They grew in popularity and included friendly Indians, so they promoted friendship between the races. Besides trading and buying items they needed, everyone had fun. They gambled and competed in games of skill—foot races, horse races, jumping contests, wrestling matches, and target shooting contests with bows and arrows and with rifles. So, you can see that once a year there were plenty of athletic activities. However, there were no teams—just one person trying to outdo all the others. I'm sure there were no written rules, although there must have been some sort of judging or refereeing to keep things fair—or at least kind of fair. The trappers would place bets on who they thought would be the winner.

Besides contests of skill, the men had other kinds of fun: storytelling, card games, singing, eating, and dancing. The only women who attended were Indians, who danced just Indian dances, so the trappers danced with one another—just as sailors had done at sea for centuries. Supplies for the trappers to buy were brought in by horses and mules from St. Louis and other places. Often the supplies included foods that they hadn't tasted in a long time, such as coffee, sugar, and flour for baking.

Jim attended many of these Mountain Fairs, and, because of his great skill with bow and arrow and with rifle, I bet he won many of the contests, although, to my surprise, he didn't boast of his triumphs in his book.

An athletic feat that Jim's book does relate is that he once ran 95 miles in a day to escape a bunch of Indians who were chasing him. If he did, he sure was one heck of an athlete. He and a Swiss trapper named Aleck Alexander were traveling on foot

The 1838 Rendezvous site near today's town of Riverton, Wyoming, on the Wind River. Indians, mountain men, and traders all camped here together in harmony (well, I suppose there were a few fights). Jim probably had fun doing athletic feats here.

when they were discovered by a band of unfriendly Indians. Jim said, "Let's run," but Aleck said he couldn't. So, Jim told Aleck to hide in some bushes while Jim took off running, figuring the Indians would chase him rather than search the bushes. That's what happened, which saved Aleck's life. Jim thought that he could run as far as a place called the Buttes, where a bunch of his buddies were camped. But, when he got there, still ahead of his pursuers, he found to his dismay that the camp was deserted—Jim's buddies had moved on. Because they hadn't found water along their route, they'd traveled another 45 miles to the closest river. Jim knew that the Indians pursuing him would be scolded by their tribe if they gave up the chase, and if they caught him they'd kill him immediately. As they came nearer, he took off running again.

He followed the tracks of his buddies. By now, he was extremely thirsty, not having had any water since he started running. At last he came within a mile of his friends' camp. The Indians saw the smoke from the campfire and knew that they'd lost the chase. At the camp, a bunch of the men mounted their horses and gave chase to the Indians, who must also have been mighty tired and thirsty. Night was fast approaching, so Jim's book mentions that most of the Indians escaped,.

Jim claimed his legs were so swollen that for the next couple of days he could barely walk. I don't doubt it. You see, I've run several 26-mile marathons, but I trained for many months, I got to drink water at aid stations along the way, and I wore good running shoes. My legs and feet were mighty sore after the 26 miles, so I find it awesome that Jim ran 95 miles with no training, no water, and no modern-day running shoes.

What about the Swiss trapper, Aleck? Well, he showed up in the camp a few days later, expecting that Jim had been killed by the Indians many miles back. He was amazed to see Jim and agreed that Jim must have run 95 miles. So, perhaps Jim's story is correct, and, if he lived today instead of 200 years ago, he'd be a super Olympic distance runner.

If Jim lived in today's world, he might also be an Olympic champion in rifle shooting or archery. Many people knew of his superb marksmanship with bow and arrow, and his

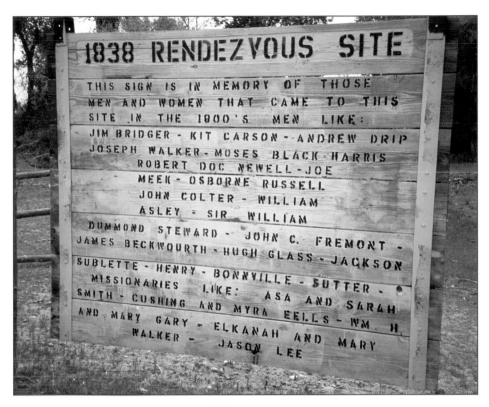

A modern-day sign at the site of the 1838 Rendezvous. You can see Jim's name on the sixth line from the bottom.

reputation as a good shot with a rifle was known through the West. But my guess is that Jim would have been good at a lot of modern-day sports if he lived now. Perhaps he'd be like another bi-racial super athlete, Tiger Woods. We'll never know, of course.

9

Jim Dodges Death
Dozens of Times

If the person in a story is almost killed but somehow miraculously survives, the story is more exciting. Well, Jim's book is crammed full of descriptions of adventures in which he lived to tell about his close calls with death. If only half of his stories are true, he was one heck of an escape artist. I'll tell you some of my favorite stories of near-death from Jim's book—and who cares if they aren't all true.

Jim was traveling back to Fort Leavenworth near Kansas City, Kansas, from Santa Fe, New Mexico, with two other men. He was supposed to join up with one of his good buddies, the famous mountain man Kit Carson, at Taos, New Mexico, but Kit never showed up. After waiting for a few days, Jim and his two companions started for Fort Leavenworth without Kit. The three men camped in the open near a group of trees.

Jim heard Indians coming and, knowing they were from the unfriendly Pawnee tribe, gathered up his camping stuff and hustled his pals and the three horses to the protection of the trees. The Pawnees arrived and set up camp just where Jim had been camping a few minutes earlier. The men and their horses needed to keep completely silent so as not to attract the attention of the Pawnees.

The Indians had killed a buffalo, so they were busy all day butchering it. To keep them from hearing or seeing the three horses, Jim and his two friends forced the horses to lie down on their sides, tied them down, and gagged each one with a cloth in its mouth so they couldn't make a sound. All day the three men and their poor horses lay still, hoping that the Pawnees wouldn't notice them. If they were discovered, the men

There were many dangers in the rugged mountains of the Wild West. That's my wife, Mary, checking out our hiking route through this beautiful country in the Sierra mountains about 30 miles from the Beckwourth Emigrant Trail.

were goners. As Jim said in his book: "I thought that day the longest I had lived through. I expect the poor animals thought so too, for they lay in one position the whole time, without food or water and without being able to whisper a complaint. At night we made good our escape and arrived at the fort without further difficulty."

In another chapter of his book Jim describes how he was a bartender in a bar where some Cheyenne Indians were sitting around together with Bull Bear, a chief of the Sioux tribe. A tall Sioux Indian, already very drunk, walked in and asked to see the Crow.

"Are you the Crow?" he asked.

"Yes," answered Jim.

"You have killed a host of [many] Sioux?" asked the stranger.

"No," replied Jim, "I have killed a host of Cheyennes but I have killed only 14 Sioux with my own hand."

The drunken Indian said to Jim, "I am a great Sioux brave. Come out, and I will kill you."

Jim knew that he could easily kill this fellow, but, if he did, he himself would immediately be killed by the watching Indians.

Jim's aggressor took off a cloth he was wearing around his waist and struck Jim in the face with it. A battle-axe was hanging from Jim's wrist, and, in a rage at being struck by the drunken Sioux, Jim raised his axe and swung it overhead to smash it into the Indian. However, the axe hit a low roof beam instead of the Sioux. Jim raised his axe again to strike a second blow, but he was restrained by the Cheyennes, who had been watching.

The Sioux chief, Bull Bear, had also seen and heard what had

Mountain men had to cross roaring streams and rivers because there were no bridges. Many of the men couldn't swim, so slipping and falling in midstream might mean death by drowning. Jim was a good swimmer, but even he might have had trouble crossing Haypress Creek, shown here, which is about an hour's drive from Jim's California ranch.

happened. He jumped up from his seat and, instead of killing Jim, Bull Bear chopped his own warrior down and hacked him to pieces after he fell. "Ugh," grunted the chief to his victim, as coolly as possible, "you ought to have been killed long ago, you bad Indian!"

All the other men in the bar had seen how Jim had been treated by the drunken Sioux, and they admired Jim for not putting up with a slap in the face. So, instead of being killed by the onlookers, Jim became a hero again.

Another brush with death that is told about in Jim's book occurred when he was with a group of mountain men traveling from St. Louis to the Rocky Mountains to spend the year trapping beavers. The best time for trapping beavers was in the spring and summer after their fur had become thick to keep the beavers warm during the cold winter. The trappers had many horses, some to ride and others to use as pack animals carrying their supplies. One night a bunch of Indians silently crept up and stole all the horses, leaving the men without any means of traveling except on foot. General Ashley, the group's leader, asked for two volunteers to travel on foot to a village of friendly Pawnee Indians and buy horses to bring them back to the group. The Indian village was estimated to be 300 miles away through wilderness with no trails. It was late October and starting to turn cold. For sure, the trip was going to be tough.

An old experienced mountaineer by the name of Moses Harris said he'd go, because he was familiar with the country and knew about how Indians lived. He also could cover long distances on foot each day, which took extreme effort. Young Jim volunteered to be the second person. Moses told Jim that, if he wasn't able to keep up the rapid pace, he would be left behind on the trail alone to die.

Jim said, "That's all right with me." So off the two went, with 25 pounds of food plus a blanket, a rifle, and ammunition for each of them.

After ten days of traveling 30 miles a day (a huge distance to walk while carrying stuff, I can assure you) they arrived at the Pawnee village. To their dismay, the village was deserted. The tribe had moved elsewhere for the winter. By then Jim and Moses were almost out of food, because they had

Traveling through the mountains in winter, Jim nearly froze or starved to death on several occasions. Frozen Wades Lake in the center of this aerial photograph is in the rugged Sierra mountains not far from Jim's ranch on the Feather River. (Photo by Woodward Payne.)

expected to get more supplies at the village, but the Pawnees had left behind no food of any kind. What were they to do? They decided to continue on, hoping to reach a trading post many miles farther on the Missouri River. After nine more days of walking, Jim was able to kill an elk so they could eat again. The elk meat quickly spoiled, so they traveled on for five more days without tasting food. Their pace had slowed considerably, because they were so tired and hungry. They'd even thrown their blankets away to save the weight of carrying them. It seemed that fatigue and starvation would soon finish them off.

When they were still about 30 miles from the trading post, Moses gave up and threw himself on the ground, saying that he couldn't go any farther. Jim saw that if he tried to help Moses along, they'd both die. So, although Jim was near death himself, he forged on toward the trading post, leaving Moses behind with no food or blanket. Jim hurried on, and a half mile after leaving Moses he heard a gunshot. Looking in the direction of the sound Jim saw two friendly Indians walking toward him. When they reached Jim they could see that he was near death, and one said, "You are dead—you no live." As best he could, Jim explained that he'd left a dying companion back on the trail. Then one of the Indians went back with Jim to where Moses lay, and the other took off for their village to bring help. Once the two travelers were safely at the village, the helpful Indians gave them cornmeal mush in small spoonfuls until both had recovered enough to eat a normal meal. Thus, both Jim and Moses escaped starvation and, after a few days' rest, were able to travel to the trading post with the Indians, who had been heading there anyway to trade.

At long last, Jim returned to St. Louis, where he met General Ashley. The general was surprised to find him alive because no word had reached the group about his and Moses's survival.

Another of Jim's many escapes from death happened when he was living with the Crows. A bunch of them were hunting buffalo. They met seven Blackfoot Indians, the Crows' worst enemies. Finding retreat cut off, the Blackfeet hastily built a sand fort from which to fight the Crows. Jim was standing, watching the two groups fight, when a bullet fired from the sand fort struck the wide blade of the hunting knife he had attached to his belt. If the bullet had landed one inch farther to the left or right, Jim would have died. The bullet hit the knife with such force, in fact, that he was knocked out and fell to the ground.

He came to quickly, and, when he got up, blood was coming from his mouth. Not knowing that the bullet had hit only his knife, he assumed it had entered a vital part of his body and that he would soon die. The Crows, who feared the same thing, carried him to their village and gathered around to watch his life end. Jim had unstrapped his knife by then. When the medicine men searched for his wound, they discovered, to their joy and surprise, that there was no bullet hole in Jim's body, only a slight black-and-blue mark. Later, the bullet was found where Jim had fallen, and it was flattened as if struck with a hammer. The Crows were wild with excitement at this discovery: they thought that Jim was bulletproof, that the bullet had been flattened as it hit his body without causing a wound or entering his body. Jim figured out what had happened, but he never let the Crows know that it was his knife blade that had flattened the bullet, not his skin.

Well, these are only a few of the dozens of stories Jim tells of his near-death experiences.

10

Jim, the Sometime Carnivore

A carnivore is an animal that eats only meat—lions, tigers, and wolves are carnivores, for example. And Jim, for the part of his life when he was a mountain man and lived with the Crows, was a carnivore, too. How come? Didn't he like vegetables?

Well, out on the trail or with the Crows, vegetables, cereals, fruits, desserts, and all those other foods were not available. Oh, I guess the Indian women gathered some roots and seeds to eat, but that's all. Riding horseback or tramping on foot over the plains and Rocky Mountains, men couldn't carry any extra weight or bulk in their packs, and food items were considered excess. When the mountain men left St. Louis for their year-long trips to the Rocky Mountains, how come they didn't take pack horses to carry all kinds of extra food? Well, they did take some horses, to carry foods such as beans and flour for biscuits. But, because there were 20 to 30 men on each of these journeys, the extra food would last only a few weeks, and from then on it was meat only.

They couldn't pick fruit from trees growing along the way because there weren't any trees. Once they got to the Rockies, there were trees, but only pines and firs, which don't grow apples. (Hmmm, if the pines don't grow apples, how'd a pineapple get its name?)

So, after they'd eaten the supplies from St. Louis, about the only things Jim and his buddies carried on the trail were a few clothes, blankets (sleeping bags hadn't been invented), rifles, pistols, ammunition, tobacco, and coffee.

During the winters, when the trappers would "hole up" in one place in the wilderness for several snowy months, there naturally was no way to get any foods that grew. For the rest of the year, the men were always on the go, so they couldn't do any farming. Nor could they buy food from farmers, because these were the days before any farmers had moved to the West. So, the trappers and explorers ate meat only. How'd you like a diet like that? Heck, they couldn't even have hamburgers because there were no buns, pickles, or ketchup.

To keep from starving, Jim and his companions had to shoot and eat wild game. They lived off deer, elk, bear, buffalo, duck, and wild turkey.

They trapped beavers to sell the beaver skins, but after skinning the animals they also sometimes would eat their meat. The tail, especially, was considered a delicacy by most trappers. I bet you've never eaten beaver, bear, elk, or buffalo. I've never tried beaver or bear, but I have eaten elk and buffalo—not bad, but they'll never replace good old beef.

On several occasions, the mountain men were in places that had no wild animals or birds to kill and eat. To keep from starving, they'd eat horses, particularly if the horse had died of starvation or exposure to a storm. However, none of the mountain men's stories describe a time so desperate that there weren't even horses to eat. If that had happened, the only thing left to eat would have been one another. (Years later, the Donner party, a group of emigrants heading to California, got snowed in by early winter storms as they were crossing the Sierra mountains. Rumors said that a few of the surviving people who hadn't yet starved, in their desperation to stay alive, ate some of the folks who had already died of starvation. Anyhow, that's a story that was never proved.)

When Jim lived with the Crows he naturally ate what they ate. The tribe would move its village at least once a year to a new place that hadn't been hunted too much. Unlike the trappers, the Crows stayed in one place for several months

Herds of buffalo were hunted by the Indians—the tribes' principal food was buffalo meat. Check out the cute little buffalo calves with their moms. These beauties live in Hot Springs State Park near Thermopolos, Wyoming. They probably are distant relatives of the buffalo the Crows hunted in this area many years ago.

during the summer, so the women could gather nuts, berries, and roots if those were available (often they weren't).

So, the Indian tribes weren't 100 percent carnivores, but meat was their main food, primarily buffalo, which in those days was plentiful where the plains tribes lived.

The first time Jim went on a buffalo hunt with the Crows, when they returned to the village and the women were cutting up the dead buffalo, a young girl gave Jim a piece of raw buffalo meat. Jim started to say, "No, thanks," but a white trapper friend who also lived with the Crows for a short time stopped him.

"Go ahead, try it," the trapper said. "Buffalo meat is good any way you get it."

So, Jim reluctantly tried a raw bloody piece of buffalo meat and discovered that it tasted OK without being cooked. Would you have tried raw buffalo? Not I!

Jim did admit that he never did like one meal that the Crows liked—half-cooked strips of dried buffalo tongue. If it was fully cooked, Jim discovered that he could eat it without throwing up, but he never liked it.

After one meal with the Crows that Jim described in his book, he praised the Crow woman who had cooked it and asked what he had eaten, pretending not to know. The woman replied that it was tongue. Now, at that time, a white buddy of Jim's who could also speak the Crow language was visiting the Crow village. He knew that Jim disliked eating tongue, so he jumped up in horror and, as a joke, shouted, "Tongue! Tongue! You have ruined his medicine [meaning good luck]! If Jim is killed in battle you will immediately be killed by the Crows because you served him tongue."

The poor woman was half dead with fear. To continue the joke, Jim sprang out of the tepee, bellowing in an imitation of a buffalo, sticking out his own tongue. and pawing the ground like a mad bear. He did this to pretend that he was removing the threat of bad luck caused by eating the tongue. At last he stopped bellowing and jumping around, and he announced that the spell caused by eating tongue had now been removed.

The large crowd of Crows who had gathered around were very angry at the poor woman on whom Jim and his friend had played this joke. The Crows never knew that Jim's antics were only in jest.

One of the Crows' specialties, served at some of their feasts, was dog meat. I know it sounds gross, but that's what the history books say. I think I'd have avoided those feasts, because it was impolite to refuse to eat the food that the Indians were serving.

What kinds of food did Jim eat while he was growing up, before he left St. Louis for his adventures, and after he returned to "civilization" when he left the Crows? Well, pretty much the same stuff you and I eat today— except that we have a few more "modern" foods like ice cream. Naturally, in those days there was no Taco Bell, McDonald's, Starbucks, Baskin-Robbins, or the like. Imagine living before ice cream was invented! I'm glad I live now, with ice cream, hot dogs, and hamburgers instead of in the old Wild West with raw buffalo, half-cooked tongue, and real dog for food!

11

Jim, the Lifesaver

Yes, Jim single-handedly saved many lives. How many? There's no way of knowing for sure, but his book describes lots of times when he prevented someone, or groups of some-ones, from dying. I don't believe that all of Jim's tales were true, but the stories are fun.

For example, in three different stories, his book tells how he saved the life of his boss, General Ashley, while Jim was with a group of trappers traveling in the Rocky Mountains. The general, who was leader of the group, kept a daily note-book of his adventures, and it does mention that several times he was saved from drowning in the Green River. The trouble is that his notebook doesn't mention who saved him. Maybe it was Jim, but you'd think that the general would have given Jim the credit in what he wrote. We'll never know.

Jim claims he also saved the general from certain death when his boss was charged by an enraged buffalo. At the last second, Jim was able to fire his rifle and kill the beast before it crushed the general. We know that Jim was an excellent shot with a rifle, so perhaps this rescue actually occurred.

On many other occasions Jim saved a bunch of lives. I won't go into detail about each, because that would take up half of this book, but I'll summarize some of the ways he saved lives—according to his book, that is.

He prevented the death of perhaps hundreds of white mountain men and pioneers by convincing the Crows that they should never kill white men. Because the Crows loved and respected Jim as their Chief, Medicine Calf, they killed only other Indians—although, after Jim left the tribe, they eventually started killing white men again. Still, thousands of pioneers traveling along the famous Oregon Trail passed through Crow country safely, although they were attacked on other tribes' lands.

One winter, when Jim traveled with a group of trappers headed for the Rocky Mountains from St. Louis, his superb hunting skills allowed him to kill some ducks, a couple of elk, and an antelope to feed his companions. Most likely this saved the men from starvation.

Jim promoted peace between warring tribes. Although he was only partly successful, the success he did have probably saved the lives of many dozens of Indians.

He tried his best to convince the United States Army not to wage war against the Crows or against any other Indian tribes either. Of course, he was far from completely successful in keeping the army from killing Indians. But whatever small success he did have at preventing attacks on various tribes saved the lives of countless Indians and, I'm sure, the lives of some soldiers as well.

Speaking of American soldiers, in the years after Jim had left the Crows, he guided many army troops through country crawling with unfriendly Indians. Because he knew the ways

The Wind River Canyon in Wyoming. Jim floated through here in 1825 with his boss, General Ashley, and a group of men in small boats carrying beaver pelts back to St. Louis. Jim claimed that he saved the general from drowning in a river like this one.

of Indians, he was able to avoid encounters between the soldiers and the Indians and prevent bloodshed for both sides.

On many occasions Jim acted as a messenger for the army. Those were the days before mail service, telephones, telegraphs, radio, or any other means of communication between military commanders. Still the generals needed to know what supplies to send to distant posts, how many troops were needed, and how one group of soldiers could coordinate with other troops to be more effective. Sometimes a messenger had to travel 300 miles between forts to carry such messages, a trip that might take three weeks. The generals wanted to send Jim on these trips, with soldiers as guards, but often the soldier guards would encounter unfriendly Indians, and a fight would break out. Sometimes the entire group of soldiers would get wiped out, so the messages they were carrying never got to their intended fort. Of course, the army officer who had sent the message didn't know that his message hadn't gotten through, and he'd impatiently wait for an answer. Then, the supplies or troops he'd requested never came.

Jim said, "Leave the guard troops here. I'm going alone as a messenger. I can travel faster, be quieter, and stay more hidden from unfriendly Indians if I go all by myself. I know how to avoid trouble."

So, Jim by himself not only delivered the important messages to the fort but also prevented lots of loss of life by insisting that he travel alone instead of with a bunch of soldiers.

On quite a few occasions after his days with the Crows were over, Jim traveled with other men through the West on trips that had nothing to do with the army. Their travels went through country populated by tribes that might or might not allow white men to pass. In his book, Jim tells of several trips where Indians opposed to intrusion on their lands stopped the travelers and threatened to kill them. Most often Jim could speak their language or at least some words, which always surprised the Indians and made them respectful of the travelers.

Jim tells of one such encounter when a bunch of Apache Indians stopped him and a traveling companion with the intent of killing the two of them. Jim told the Apache group's leader to shut-up—that he himself was an Indian chief and would talk only with another chief, not with some upstart group leader who was not a chief of all the Apaches.

Evidently the group's leader was so impressed by Jim's commanding tone that he did shut up and took the travelers to his chief in the nearby Apache village.

Jim greeted the Apache chief as an equal and explained that he was a Crow chief but was now living with the white men, so that was why he wasn't dressed like a Crow. Jim did have his chief's medallion hung around his neck, and he showed it to the Apache chief.

The chief was so pleased to be visited by another chief that, instead of having Jim and his buddy killed, he honored them, gave them food, and sent them on their way with praise from the Apaches.

Yes, Jim saved a lot of lives, including his own. Hooray for Jim!

12

The Disaster Jim Couldn't Stop

During the time Jim lived with the Crow Indians (as I described in Chapter 5) the tribe reached the height of its success. But, like a football team winning the Superbowl or a baseball team winning the World Series, a tribe that rises to the top can expect a fall from that summit—sooner or later.

That's just what happened to the Crows, and Jim saw it coming but was powerless to prevent it. Wait a minute—couldn't Jim have stopped the most successful tribe on the plains from falling into decline by proper leadership? Did other tribes become more powerful instead?

Sadly, all the plains and Rocky Mountain tribes faced the same decline. There wasn't just one cause. A bunch of causes contributed to the problem, some more than others. In fact, causes started while Jim was chief, but most happened after he left the tribe. When serving as chief Jim saw that the tribe was bound to decline in the future and that he couldn't prevent the

Buffalo were hunted almost to extinction, depriving the Indians of their main source of food. Finally the government stopped hunters from killing the last few buffalo, so they were able to multiply and did not die out completely. However, the law forbidding buffalo hunting was too late to save many of the tribes.

loss. One major problem was especially foreseen by Jim. In his book he explains:

> It is a conclusion forced upon my mind that within half a century [actually, it took a lot less than 50 years] the race of buffalos [on which all the plains tribes relied for food and hides for clothes, tepees, weapons, and even boats] will be extinguished on this continent. Then farewell to the red man for he must also become extinct unless he applies himself to the cultivation of the soil, which is beyond the bound of probability. The incessant [never-ending] demand for robes has slain thousands of these noble beasts of the prairie until the Indians themselves begin to see the end of the buffalo. . . .

Doubtless when that time arrives, much of the land which they now roam over will be under the white man's cultivation, which will extend inland from both oceans. The red man's doom is apparent. It is a question of time, and not very long either; but the result, as I view it, is a matter of certainty.

A strict agreement by all tribes to conserve the buffalo might have helped a bit, but Jim was in no position to tell tribes other than the Crows what to do. True, he was well respected by the other plains and Rocky Mountain tribes because they knew what a great leader he was for the Crows, but they had their own chiefs to follow.

Jim did try, unsuccessfully, to get the Crows to adopt white men's ways to survive. Instead of moving their tepees from place to place as they followed the buffalo herds, he said they could use axes to cut trees to build permanent houses. Then they could learn how to farm and use plows for farming. He told them they could trade buffalo hides to the white traders in exchange for axes and plows. But, no matter how hard Jim tried to explain these things to the Crows, they didn't want to switch from being hunters in movable villages of tepees to being farmers settling down in one place.

There was nothing Jim could do to stop white men from moving into the Indians' territory and hunting grounds. Displacing Indians from their lands had started many years before, even before George Washington became our first president. The United States government, instead of trying to stop it, in many cases actually encouraged the takeover of Indian land.

Two other events sped up the land grabs. The first was the

As the emigrants traveled through Indian territory in covered wagons, some decided not to go all the way to California or Oregon. They took over Indian land and killed many buffalo, deer, and other animals that the Indians relied on for food. Tribes declined as their land and hunting grounds were claimed by emigrants.

building of the transcontinental railroad (called the "iron horse" by the Indians), which brought more emigrants more quickly from the eastern part of the country to the West. Second, the discovery of gold in California in 1848 resulted in the gold rush. In 1849 thousands of men called forty-niners flocked to California to find gold. Although most of them merely passed through the Indians' lands on their way, others, seeing good land for farming, stayed and took over the tribes' hunting grounds.

Could Jim have led Crow war parties to attack the white settlers who were forcing the Indians from of their land? After all, he was very successful leading Crow warriors against other tribes. Well, Jim had no appetite for attacking his fellow Americans, and, besides, he knew that the U.S. army would come to the aid of the settlers, and the Indians would get slaughtered.

Another major cause of decline for all the tribes, except the Crows, was booze, which they called "firewater." Many modern sources say that Indians are particularly attracted to drinking whiskey, which can make them violently drunk. Alcoholism caused much suffering in the tribes. As increasing numbers of braves took to firewater (history books about Jim don't mention drinking by the women) the tribe became less able to function efficiently.

The Crows escaped the curse of booze for quite a while, because when Jim was chief he declared, "Crows, you shall drink no whiskey." After he left the tribe, many of the men no longer stayed away from alcohol.

Years after Jim had left the Crows, he was a trader of goods to various tribes. The Indians exchanged goods in trade; no money was involved. Jim would take buffalo robes in exchange for items the Indians needed such as rifles, ammunition, pots, and knives. Unfortunately the item the braves desired most was firewater. They would trade goods for whiskey, drink it immediately, and get very drunk. Once drunk, they did the rest of their trading in no condition to realize that the traders were often cheating them, giving them worthless items in exchange for good buffalo robes.

At first, when Jim was a trader, he refused to trade whiskey to the Indians, because he knew that it would contribute to each tribe's downfall. But, sad to say, his book tells that he finally changed his mind:

> I was in no position to prohibit the introduction of
> white man's firewater; if I had refused to trade it to
> the Indians, plenty more traders would have fur-
> nished it to them; and my conscientious scruples
> [good morals] would benefit the Indians none and
> would deprive my embarrassed employer a very
> considerable source of profit . . . . If a man wants
> a good price for the sale of his soul to the devil,
> let him engage in the liquor business among the
> Indian nations of the Rocky Mountains.

I suppose any of us might have done what Jim did, but he wasn't proud of himself for dealing in firewater.

Disease also wiped out many Indians. As has happened around the world many times since white men started explor ing the globe in sailing ships, they unknowingly carried fatal diseases to native populations. The explorers had developed immunity to these illnesses, but the local people had none, so they died by the thousands.

Many Indian children got sick and died of whooping cough (which today can be prevented and cured) but the biggest killer was smallpox. Some tribes were reduced in half by this fatal disease. Eventually, doctors learned about inoculation— giving people a small bit of the disease germ, not enough to make them sick but enough so that their bodies would build up protection against the disease; then, if they caught the dis- ease, they wouldn't die from it. Smallpox vaccinations became widely accepted, so the disease no longer spread, but that hap- pened too late to save the lives of thousands of Indians.

An awful thing happened to Jim regarding smallpox. He was falsely accused of giving the disease to the Indians after he

Ruts were created by covered wagons crossing over soft rock along the Oregon Trail in Wyoming. The large number of emigrants traveling to the West contributed to the decline of most of the plains and Rocky Mountain tribes.

returned from a visit to St. Louis. It has been proved that Jim did not do this, but a man who disliked Jim spread the false rumor. Sadly, Jim's great reputation was severely damaged by this lie.

One final cause of tribal decline that Jim tried to stop but couldn't was the constant war between many of the tribes, whether they lived on the plains or in the Rocky Mountains. Braves of each tribe lived to attack and kill another tribe's braves and take their scalps. Warring was so much a part of what they always did and was such a big part of their culture that declaring peace between tribes was impossible. The Crows, under Jim's leadership, suffered less than any other tribe from the death of its warriors in battle. Jim had taught them better fight tactics and got them better weapons: rifles instead of bows and arrows. However, other tribes later learned to fight the way Jim had taught the Crows. In the end, even the poorest tribes acquired better weapons. So the slaughter of Indians in wars between the tribes was faster.

Of course, braves weren't killed only by opposing tribes. The U.S. army also did in many Indians. Most were merely trying to protect their tribal lands from incoming white settlers. Jim was largely able to protect the Crows from this slaughter by pleading with the army not to attack "his" tribe, but he wasn't successful in protecting other tribes from the might of the soldiers.

Years after Jim's death, the Crows finally were pushed onto the 2 1/2 million acre reservation on which they now reside in southern Montana. There are about 10,000 tribal members alive today, so the tribe has become larger during the past 100 years.

13

Jim, the Adventurous Traveler

It would take a huge book over an inch thick to tell you about all of Jim's travels. No records were kept of who did the most traveling across the North American continent during the first 66 years of the 1800s (Jim's lifetime). But if someone had kept them, Jim Beckwourth might have been the record holder. Another Jim, Jim Bridger, who was a good buddy of "our" Jim's and a wide-ranging mountain man, might have argued that he had out-traveled our superstar.

Even more spectacular than the total miles he traveled or the number of trips he took is the fact that many of his travels were through uncharted wilderness. His first big trip, when Jim was seven or eight and his family moved from Virginia to St. Louis, was probably on a wagon road. But after that, a lot of his travels for the next 30 years were over land without roads or even trails.

Wilderness travel was dangerous and slow. The dangers included hostile Indians, snow storms and foul weather, starvation—because in many places there were no animals or birds to kill and eat, bear attacks, and accidents such as falling off a bucking horse.

One of the dangers you and I would certainly face, but which was no big deal for Jim, was getting lost. With no maps, few known routes, and plenty of unknown wild mountains, many early explorers died by getting lost. Jim had an extraordinary sense of direction. He had the ability to find a good route through mountains without any path to follow or any previous knowledge about the area. His super memory allowed him

Independence Rock in Wyoming. It was Independence Day (the Fourth of July) in 1830 when the first emigrants' covered wagons arrived here along the Oregon Trail. The travelers celebrated the nation's birthday and carved their names in the soft rock, as many more did in later years. Jim passed here several times in his travels.

to follow a route someone had told him about weeks, months, or even years earlier. Even if many years had passed since he had been over a remote route, he could take that same route again and remember it exactly. Many fellow mountain men agreed that Jim was better at guiding than any other mountain man.

Journeys in the old Wild West were slow. You see, these were the days before cars, planes, or even trains. Emigrants moving west from St. Louis or other Missouri cities traveled in covered wagons pulled by horses or oxen. Traveling all day, they could cover only a few miles before the animals were tired out. The emigrants' trip from Missouri to California might take as much as six months.

The mountain men traveling to the Rocky Mountains from St. Louis could move faster than covered wagons because they rode horses. Even so, their horses didn't gallop the way you see in cowboy movies. Galloping tires a horse out quickly. A man who wants to ride a horse all day has to walk the animal, not run. So even horseback trips would take two to three months to reach the Rocky Mountains.

On the way west, many a traveler had his horse stolen by Indians (Indians were expert at stealing horses from other tribes so they excelled at stealing from white men). Even if travelers kept their horses from being stolen, the men would often wind up walking because their horses had starved or fallen sick and died when winter storms made grazing impossible.

When Jim was with the Crow Indians he went on many trips to fight neighboring tribes. These travels would last from a week to more than a month and cover hundreds of miles while the braves searched for the tribe they wanted to attack. You see, tribes moved around a lot. It wasn't easy to know their

Bent's Fort in southeastern Colorado today is a replica (copy) of the original fort, which had crumbled away. Jim worked and also occasionally stopped at the original fort on his travels through the area.

exact location at a particular time. So, sometimes the Indians "on the warpath" had to wander all around before discovering the whereabouts of their foe.

After Jim left the Crows, his big travels really began. I've tried to make a list of all his travels. But that's tough to do, because, for many of his trips, I had to rely on what Jim described in his book—and, as we know, Jim's book was quite inaccurate. Also, there are "holes" in the accounts of his travels where there's no clue about where he was for several months.

Many of Jim's trips later in life were made because he'd been hired as a messenger by the army or the government. Usually each trip took several weeks, covered hundreds of miles, and took him to many different parts of the Wild West.

One reason Jim could make so many dangerous trips—and other messengers could not—was that he was a "retired" Crow chief (see Chapter 5 for that story). Not only did he know the ways of the unfriendly Indians, but he also was a hero among all the tribes of the plains and Rocky Mountains. He was honored and respected by Indians everywhere, even if they weren't Crows. So, if Indians discovered him while he was traveling, he wasn't harmed. Naturally, the fact that he could speak so many Indian languages was also a big help in allowing him to deal with tribes he met on his travels.

Jim made many trips as a guide for the army or the government as well as for other groups of travelers. His knowledge of the territory and how to best get from one place to another was always useful. His most fun as a guide must have been when, in 1850, he led the first group of emigrants over the trail he had pioneered, coming into California. (You can read about his trail in Chapter 19.) Part of the reason he built the trail in the first place was not just to make money but also to offer the poor, tired emigrants an easier way to reach their goal, California.

Near the end of this book, in Appendix 2, I've tried to list in correct order all of Jim's excursions. Just glance at that list, if you wish to see how extensive his travels were. Here, I'll just tell you a little bit about two of his adventures.

When he left the Crows for the last time, he returned to St. Louis. Not being the kind of guy to just sit around, he began looking for something new to do. The economy was in bad shape and jobs were scarce. A friend suggested that Jim talk to General Edmund Gaines, who was recruiting men to go to Florida with the army to fight the Seminole Indians. Florida, with its warm weather, sounded like an interesting change from the cold Rocky Mountains. Besides, Jim was always eager for adventure. He rounded up a bunch of his out-of-work mountain man buddies, and they all traveled to Tampa Bay, Florida, by boat.

They began their trip on a paddle-wheel riverboat, going down the Mississippi River to New Orleans. Then they took a sailing ship to Florida. Jim had never been on the ocean (actually the Gulf of Mexico) before, and, to his dismay, when major storms occurred at sea, this big hearty outdoorsman got very seasick. Because the mountain men had no experience at sea, they put all their horses together in a large room in the bottom of the ship. When the storms hit, the poor horses were tumbled about and many were crushed or so severely injured, that they had to be thrown overboard. The voyage took longer

El Pueblo was the first building built in the City of Pueblo, Colorado. This replica is adjacent to a soon-to-be-built park that will be named Jim Beckwourth Plaza. Jim was one of the city's founders.

Jim probably visited the old pueblo (Indian village) at Taos, New Mexico, many times because it was actively inhabited by Indians in the mid-1800s. The original pueblo is still in use today.

than expected, and they ran out of horse feed, so more of the horses died of starvation.

In Jim's book he claims that he became captain of the troop of mountain men in Florida. This was one of Jim's typical "overstatements." Research shows that he wasn't even a soldier, just a civilian employee of the army without any rank. His pay records say that he was an "express rider" (his old messenger job). After the biggest battle of the Seminole War, which was won by the United States troops, Jim was chosen by General Zachary Taylor to carry news of the victory to Tampa Bay. General Taylor later became the 12th president of the United States.

After the big battle, the army had little for Jim to do, and he disliked the humid weather, so he returned to St. Louis. He'd spent about ten months in Florida. From then on, some folks referred to him as Captain Beckwourth, and he never bothered to correct them.

When he was 44 years old, Jim had another interesting trip I'd like you to know about. He became tired of his many adventures in the conflicts between Mexico and Texas, so he decided to find something new and different to do. He headed west to California, where he'd never been before, arriving in Pueblo de los Angeles, which later became Los Angeles. History books show that Jim was one of 200 foreigners (not Mexicans—California was part of Mexico then) to visit California in 1844. Of these, only 100 were regarded as "pioneer residents." The name James Beckwourth is fourth on this list of the original 100 residents of Los Angeles. I enjoy the thought of Jim being one of the very first Americans in what is now one of the world's largest metropolitan areas.

In Pueblo de Angeles Jim opened a store, but that venture lasted less than a year before he moved on to where there was more excitement. Of course, adventure and excitement were what Jim liked best.

14

How Jim Looked and Dressed

You can see photos of Jim as an adult in this book. There are no photos or written descriptions of Jim while he was growing up, so you'll just have to imagine what he looked like. You see, the camera hadn't been invented when Jim was a boy.

After his school years, when he worked for the blacksmith he developed pretty good muscles. As a blacksmith he used a heavy hammer all day to pound on metal hot from the forge. He certainly didn't need to build muscles in a gym or work-out room by lifting weights or using weight machines, which weren't even invented until many years later. His blacksmith work was enough to give him bulging muscles.

When Jim reached adulthood he stood six feet tall. That doesn't sound particularly tall today, but people were a lot shorter in the early 1800s, so he was taller than most men. His eyes were dark and looked fearsome when he got angry.

We don't have any photographs of Jim when he lived

Drawing of Jim dressed in his mountain man clothing. (Courtesy of the Nevada Historical Society.)

with the Crows, but the drawing in Chapter 5 does show how he probably looked in his Crow Indian clothing. And there are lots of written descriptions of his looks and dress in those years.

Indian men wore their hair long, so Jim let his grow. In his book he said it descended all the way to his hips. Sometimes he'd wear it in Indian fashion, in braids with colored ribbons woven into them.

His clothing was all made of animal skins, mostly deer but also some antelope and mountain sheep. His Indian wives ornamented his clothes with colored beads and bits of other things. When he dressed like this, it was almost impossible to know that he wasn't an Indian.

His book tells this story about a time when Jim in Indian dress joined some Crows on a trip to Fort Clark, to trade for supplies:

> Toward the conclusion of the business, one of my tribe inquired in his own language for "Be-has-I-pe-hish-a." The clerk could not understand what he wanted and there was none of the article in sight for the Indian to point out. He [the clerk] at length called Kipp [the trading post owner] to see if he could determine the Indian's meaning. I then said in English, "Gentlemen, that Indian wants scarlet cloth." If a bombshell had exploded in the fort, they could not have been more astonished. "Ah," said one of them, "you speak English! Where did you learn it?"
>
> "With the white man."
>
> "How long were you with the whites?"
>
> "More than twenty years."
>
> "Where did you live with them?"
>
> "In St. Louis."
>
> "In St. Louis! In St. Louis! You have lived twenty years in St. Louis?"

Photo of Jim in 1855 when he was 55 years old and living on his California ranch. Even though he's all dressed up with a bow tie, he wanted the photographer to make sure his bowie knife was clearly visible. (Courtesy of the Nevada Historical Society.)

Then they scanned me closely from head to foot and Kipp said, "If you have lived twenty years in St. Louis, I'll swear you are no Crow."

"No I am not."

"Then what may be your name?"

"My name in English is James Beckwourth."

"Good heavens! Why, I have heard your name mentioned a thousand times. You were supposed to be dead and were so reported by Captain Sublette."

"I am not dead, as you see. I still move and breathe." All this conversation was unintelligible to my Crow brethren, who were evidently proud to see a Crow talk so fluently with a white man.

JAMES P. BECKWOURTH IN CITIZEN'S DRESS.

A drawing of Jim that appeared in his book, showing how he looked as a middle-aged man in formal clothing. Yes, Jim looked good all dressed up, and his manners and speech were just as good as his looks. (Courtesy of the Nevada Historical Society.)

Jim loved jewelry, and the history books tell us that he wore gold chains, fancy buttons, and even earrings—his ears were pierced in several places. (And you thought guys wearing earrings was a modern-day invention, didn't you?)

When he was a Crow chief and went into a battle against other tribes, he'd wear his chief's outfit, which included a headdress made of feathers, and war paint on his face. In battle he carried a round shield made of tough animal skin, which could deflect an arrow, though it wouldn't stop a bullet. Every warrior had his own markings painted on his shield, and it became a personal possession of great value to him. Jim's had a crescent moon with a green bird in the center and a star on each side, plus feathers hanging from its edges.

Jim also wore a chief's necklace, which one writer described as a perforated bullet with a long oblong bead on each side of it, suspended around his neck with a long thin strip of animal skin. Later in life, after he'd left the Crows, he switched to a necklace made of an 1800 silver dollar, which he said marked the date of his birth (but in his book, Jim said that he was born in 1798—I'm confused).

Later in life, when Jim had settled in California, he occasionally visited San Francisco. For such trips he'd dress like prominent San Francisco residents did. His manners made him seem like a perfectly refined gentleman rather than a raw outdoorsman. It takes a man of great ability to go from slavery to chief of the Crow nation to the high society of San Francisco with ease and gain acceptance by each group.

As Jim grew old, his hard life started to show, although one writer who knew him at that time said, "He is now 62 years of age but looks scarce 50, hale, hearty and straight as an arrow." Nonetheless, his body and face had plenty of scars from battle

The picture of Jim used on the front of a 29-cent U.S. postage stamp issued in 1993 as part of a commemorative sheet of 20 different stamps titled Legends of the West. *This is how he probably dressed in cold weather during his travels after he no longer lived with the Crow tribe. (James Beckwourth stamp image © 1993 United States Postal Service. All rights reserved. Used with permission.)*

wounds. He couldn't do the many physical things he'd done all his life—but, heck, that's true of all folks as they get old, isn't it? It's a rare athlete who, once he or she is 40 years old, can effectively play professional sports.

The pictures in this book do a good job of showing you how Jim looked and dressed after he left the Crows. I've searched a lot of places to find these pictures—they're all I found. Luckily we have these. I particularly like the small statue I have of Jim in his mountain man dress. He looks like a pretty tough hombre, doesn't he?

15

Finding Jim's Faults

Was our superstar a perfect person? Far from it! Few famous people are without flaws. Well, that could be said of all of us, right? So, what did Jim do that wasn't so super?

Well, I guess the worst thing Jim did was to go into battle against other tribes with his fellow Crows. Battle with spears, axes, bows and arrows, and guns is usually pretty awful. So, why did Jim do it? I suppose it was because he was trying to fit in with the Crow tribe. He wanted to become a good warrior and to do what Crow braves did. According to Jim's book, he often took part in small groups of Crows who went on the warpath, as going to fight other tribes was called then.

Now, you probably know that Indian warriors attacked only other men—women and children were never part of their battles. And, as I mention in Chapter 5, the Crows didn't fight with the mountain men or the emigrants passing through on their way to California. I suppose Jim could have stayed in camp and never ventured out with the warring parties. But then he would never have become chief and would never have done all the good things he did for the tribe as their leader. Should he

95

Jim's War Shield: Indian shields were often made of weasel hide, which is very tough (it might stop an arrow but not a bullet). The weasel was admired by the Indians because it is a fierce fighting animal and was believed to be good war "medicine." (Drawn by Tom DeMund.)

have become a warrior? I don't think we should be his judge.

Jim also was a thief—big time. However, he stole only one kind of thing: horses. The Indians didn't think that stealing horses was wrong. That was just one of the things, besides making war and hunting, that grown-up male Indians did. Many tribes believed that stealing horses was something to be proud of. So, while Jim lived with the Crows he became an accomplished horse thief. It took a lot of skill to drive off a bunch of horses belonging to another tribe without being caught. (A horse was one of very few things a male Indian could own; the others were his few clothes, robes, warring equipment, and tepee.) So, it doesn't seem particularly awful that Jim joined with other Crows in stealing horses, because the Indians from whom they had been stolen would try to steal them back. Sounds kind of like a game, to me.

Jim was a rebel against the government at one time, too—the Mexican government, that is. Many years after he had returned to live with white men, he participated in the California Bear Flag Rebellion. You see, settlers who had moved to California from the eastern part of the United States tried to take over California from the Mexicans who had governed it for many years. The settlers' goal was to make California a separate nation apart from the United States and from Mexico. Their flag had a grizzly bear on it—so their fight was called the Bear Flag Rebellion. During the rebellion, Jim helped wipe out a lot of Mexicans so that white Californians, greedy for land, could take over the Mexicans' property.

Jim used his expertise as a horse thief to steal a herd of 2,000 horses from a Mexican ranch in California. He herded them to New Mexico, where he sold them to the U.S. army. The army then used some of the horses to travel to California to put an end to the Bear Flag Rebellion against Mexico. It was said that Jim used the money he got from the sale to buy a hotel in Santa Fe, which he ran for a while.

So, I guess in this instance, and probably others, he was indeed a thief. However, in all the stuff written about Jim during and after his life, there is no mention of him stealing anything but horses.

Another fault that Jim had was the way he treated his wives. (Yes, he had a bunch of wives; you'll read about them in Chapter 17.) So, was he physically rough on women? No, but he did some things that weren't kind—mainly ignoring his wives. While living with the Crows, he treated his Indian wives the way other Crow husbands treated theirs. The Crow women were supposed to gather plant food, cook it, serve it, do all the housework (I mean, tepee work), make the clothes, take care of and raise the children, and be good bed companions when needed. In other words, the women did everything but hunt, go on warring parties, and steal horses. When Jim left the tribe to live in the white world again, he left his wives and kids behind. No one knows if he visited them or kept in touch. All Crow women were expected to carry on when a husband was away or had been killed. Another brave (often a relative) would help out by teaching the boys of the missing husband how to hunt, steal horses, and fight other tribes.

What else was a stain on Jim's reputation? He was a liar! Well, there are lies that discredit or harm other people, and then there are lies that just make a story sound more exciting than it really was. As I said in Chapter 0, Jim's book and the stories he told to other mountain men around the evening campfire certainly contained lots of exaggeration, but so what? Did these lies hurt other people, or did they merely entertain Jim's listeners and readers? My take on the matter is that Jim's exaggerations didn't do any harm. Although each might be called a lie, because it wasn't exactly correct, that doesn't put them in the same category as a deceit that causes harm to someone. What do you think?

Another item that might be considered a Jim Beckwourth fault was his hot temper. Remember how he got into a fight with his first boss, George Casner, the owner of the blacksmith shop where Jim worked?

Jim also got into a shouting match with General Ashley, who was his boss on several of the year-long trips from St. Louis to the Rocky Mountains. One day he got angry when the general had some harsh words for him. But telling your boss off is never a wise thing to do. Although Jim and the general later became friends, it took a while to get over their quarrel.

In his book Jim describes several other times when his quick temper flared up, but he always explained that he had a good excuse for his rage. We all might say the same in writing our life's story. I bet he was right most of the time.

Perhaps, as you read this chapter, you might think that Jim was an awful person. Absolutely not. He had hundreds of good friends who respected and liked him. Certainly these people wouldn't have liked Jim if he'd been a crummy person. Let's forgive Jim for not being perfect, because not one of us is.

16

Jim's Jobs— a World Record?

Jim might have held the world record for doing more different jobs than anyone else in his day, if anyone had been keeping records. I've made a list of his jobs, which are described in various old books written about him. I counted 40 kinds of jobs, not counting the unpaid work he had while he lived with the Crow Indian tribe. Jim was never out of work—well, almost never. That was because he had so many talents. He always did more than he was required to do and did it better!

I won't describe his jobs in every detail but merely list the 40 with a brief comment on each. These are more or less in the order in which Jim did them.

1. Blacksmith. In his first job, Jim learned to make things of metal. The blacksmith would heat the metal in a forge (hot fire) until it was red hot and soft; then he'd beat it with a heavy hammer to shape it into whatever he wanted to make. Jim often made horseshoes, which were nailed to

the bottoms of horses' hooves. (No ouch, because a hoof is made out of the same sort of stuff as your fingernails and toenails—it doesn't hurt you to cut those, does it?)

2. Hunter. Yes, hunting was a job. Miners and trappers lived mostly on the meat of wild animals. They hired a person like Jim, who was a good shot with a rifle, to kill deer, buffalo, antelope, ducks, and wild turkeys for food.

3. Miner. Jim worked in the lead mines of Fever River (now called Galena), Illinois.

4. Valet (pronounced vah-lay). Jim acted as a personal helper to his boss, General William Ashley.

5. Wrangler. A wrangler takes care of horses. This was one of Jim's jobs on his trips to the Rocky Mountains with General Ashley.

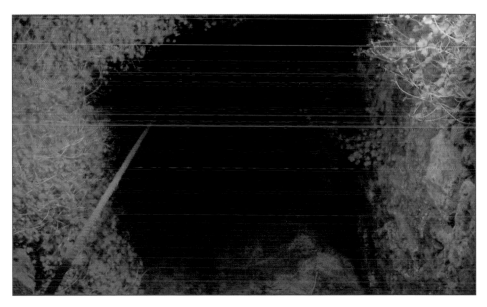

Looking down into the vertical shaft of one of the lead mines in Fever River (now Galena), Illinois. (Yes, I know this is an ugly photo, but, hey, it was the best I could do.) Jim worked in one of these Fever River mines when he was 22 years old.

The long-gone Denver store that Jim owned with Pike Vasquez in 1859
was located in the middle of this grassy soccer field, used by the University
of Colorado—Denver campus today. That unusual building in the
background is the Tivoli Brewery built in 1882. Just to right of this photo,
a block away, is the Pepsi Center, where the Denver Nuggets professional
basketball team plays.

6. Trapper. Jim spent several years, off and on, trapping beavers in the Rocky Mountains. After he sold the beaver skins, they were sent to the eastern United States for making hats. (Look at Appendix 1 after the last chapter in this book to read about how the beavers were trapped.)

7. Packer. When the trapping season was over, the beaver skins had to be packed into bundles of 60 skins each, for shipping back to St. Louis. Jim earned $25 per month in this job.

8. Trapper Group Leader. General Ashley appointed Jim leader of a group of 80 trappers when he was very young—only 25 years old. None but the very best men became leaders.

9. Trader. The Indians of many different tribes traded buffalo and beaver skins for things they needed. Trading post owners hired traders made these deals with the Indians. Because Jim spoke so many Indian languages he became an expert trader.

10. Trapping Company Owner. Jim hired and paid Indians to trap beavers for him. He sold the beaver skins to the trading post operators. Jim could make much more money by hiring others than by doing all the trapping by himself.

11. Trading Post Agent. Jim's trading skills with the Indians were so good that he was hired by a post owner to oversee several trading posts. Jim then hired a man to run each post. He continually traveled from one post to another, making sure that they were doing OK.

12. Fort Builder. Forts were built to protect supplies and pioneers from unfriendly Indians. Jim was hired to supervise the building of several forts in the Rocky Mountains. Forts typically had 18-foot-high walls made of logs.

13. Army Captain. Jim got together a bunch of his buddies to travel from St. Louis to Florida to fight the Seminole Indians. In his book, he claims that he was made the head military officer of this group, but others say he wasn't (see Chapter 13).

14. Mule Skinner. You might think that a mule skinner skins mules. Nope, he doesn't. As an employee of the U.S. army in Florida, Jim was hired to get mules ready to haul army wagons. It would be another 70 years before trucks were invented to do the hauling.

15. Teamster. Today a member of the Teamsters' Union drives a big truck, but in those days teamsters drove wagons pulled by teams of horses or mules. Jim was paid $50 a month to work as a teamster, which probably included some mule skinning.

16. Courier. A courier carries messages from one person to another. Jim was hired by the U.S. army many times to carry important messages from one army fort to another. The army considered him one of its best couriers.

17. News carrier. Being a news carrier was like being a courier except that, instead of going between military forts, Jim visited villages to give the townspeople news. There were no newspapers, phones, radios, TVs, or computer Internet

The store at Bent's Fort in southeastern Colorado where Jim worked in 1840. Yes, it looks new, because it is a modern replica (copy) of the original store.

sites to spread news, so carriers like Jim were occasionally hired to do the job in person.

18. Trading Post Builder. Because Jim was so good at building things, William Bent hired him to build and establish several new trading posts on the eastern slope of the Rocky Mountains.

19. Mailman. When the U.S. mail first started, delivery of a letter took a long time. Mail had to be carried by a rider on a horse—the trucks and airplanes that carry today's mail hadn't yet been invented. For a while, Jim rode his horse between San Francisco and Monterey, California, carrying the U.S. mail. Another time, he was a mail carrier between Santa Fe, New Mexico, and Fort Leavenworth, Kansas.

20. City Founder. For each city in America, somebody had to be the first person to live there and be its founder. Jim was among the first Americans to live in what is today Pueblo, Colorado. Located 110 miles south of Denver, Pueblo now has over 100,000 people. So, Jim helped start a city that has grown into Colorado's fourth-largest community. Of course, he didn't get paid for this, so perhaps it wasn't really a job.

21. Store Owner. Jim had one of the first stores in Stockton, California. His store sold clothes to the gold miners, and it was actually located in a tent because there were no buildings for rent in the early days of Stockton. Other places where Jim owned stores were Denver, Colorado, and Taos, New Mexico. The long-gone store in Denver that he co-owned with A. Pike Vasquez is now the site of a University of Colorado—Denver soccer field.

22. Spy. When Jim lived with the Crow Indians, he learned how to observe the enemy without being seen. The army

Site where a huge amount of gold was discovered in 1851 by a couple of prospectors in California. Jim also traveled through this area looking for gold. He didn't find any but he did discover the pass over the Sierra mountains that gave him the idea for his emigrant trail.

used Jim's spying talents to bring information to army officers about what their opponents were doing.

23. Hotel Owner. Jim and a partner bought and ran a hotel in Santa Fe, New Mexico, many years before New Mexico became one of the states of the Union. Jim reported that the hotel was very profitable.

24. Salesman in a Store. Although at several different times Jim owned his own stores, he also was hired by other store owners to be a salesperson. He must have been a good salesman, because his salary was much higher than those of other men and women working in the same store.

25. Army Guide. Jim knew the trails of the Rocky Mountains because he had helped create them. The army was often clueless about how to get from one place to another. Jim

was hired to guide soldiers to where they needed to go. He knew the safest and easiest way—the army didn't.

26. Interpreter. Jim was of great value to the army and to many other travelers because he knew so many Indian languages. He could tell a white man what an Indian was saying and tell the Indian what the white person was saying.

27. Horse Thief. Stealing horses is a job? It was for Jim. During the U.S. government's war with Mexico, he stole horses from the Mexicans and sold them to the U.S. army. He became an expert at horse stealing during his years with the Crow tribe.

28. Cook. During the U.S. war with Mexico, Jim was also hired by one of the leaders to be this personal cook. I'd guess this meant that Jim knew how to do a good job of preparing meals.

29. Saloon Owner. As part of his hotel business, Jim operated a bar. His saloon quickly became a favorite place for town folks and visitors to have a drink. He was reputed to have the best selection of booze in New Mexico.

30. Army Supply Provider. Jim knew how to get things that the army needed because he could speak so many languages and knew so many people all over the Wild West. Very few people could provide this service as well as Jim could.

31. Gambler. Jim was terrific at card games—"one of the best in the West." One night he won several thousand dollars, which was an awesome amount of money in those days. He treated the whole town to drinks and gave the rest away to the poor and to needy miners, so he was broke again a few days later.

32. Card Dealer. In a place where people gambled, men were hired to deal the cards and run the games. One of the

most popular games was monte. Players bet on the color of the card the dealer would turn up from the deck. Jim had the reputation of being one of the all-time best monte dealers.

33. Mine Crew Boss. When the gold rush to California was at its peak, Jim was 49 years old. He didn't care to spend long days at hard labor mining gold, so he hired a bunch of Indians to do the hard work for him. He supplied all the tools, and when he sold the newly mined gold, he split the profits with the Indians.

34. Farm Manager. Jim liked "action" too much to live for many years as a farmer. But when he was 60 years old he did manage a farm near Denver for his old business partner A. Pike Vasquez.

35. Farmer. After running the farm for Vasquez, Jim decided he wanted to try farming for himself, so he bought land in south Denver (today, a freeway, Interstate 25, runs right through the land that was Jim's farm). Some people have said that Jim became the first farmer in Denver. Of course, there are no farms right in Denver today.

36. Trail Builder. Jim planned the route of the now famous Beckwourth Emigrant Trail (read all about it in Chapter 19) and hired a work crew to help him cut trees and make the road.

37. Rancher and Cowboy. After Jim completed his emigrant trail, he started a cattle ranch nearby, about where the small town of Beckwourth, California, is today.

38. Indian Agent. The U.S. government hired people to be its agents in dealing with the Indians. Years after Jim had left the Crow tribe, he established a close relationship with the Cheyenne tribe. He'd often helped the Cheyennes when

The pueblo at Taos, New Mexico, is near where Jim owned a store in 1842.

they had problems with white settlers, and the Indians trusted him. So Jim was a logical choice to be hired as an Indian Agent to deal with the Cheyennes on behalf of the U.S. government.

39. Author. In Chapter 0 I told about the book written about Jim's life. He didn't actually do the writing, but he told his life story to this guy Thomas Bonner who actually drafted the book. Still, Jim wrote lots of notes to help him with the story, so he definitely can be considered the coauthor.

40. Treaty Maker. Because Jim knew the Crow Indians so well, he was asked to represent the U.S. government in negotiating a peace treaty with the Crows to prevent a war. He succeeded (but read Chapter 20 to find out what happened to him after the treaty was signed).

In his book Jim stated that he hated to be inactive. He always wanted to be doing something. Looking at the above list, you can tell that he got his wish.

17

A Man of Many Wives

I've known some people who have been married twice, or even three or four times. Perhaps you have, too. However, being married to two people at the same time—that's not OK in the United States. It's illegal and was illegal even before Jim was born. Yet Jim had many wives. From all the stuff I've read about him, I've made a list of 11 wives. Now, some of the Indian wives Jim tells about in his book are probably exaggerations. We'll never know if Jim's claim to 11 wives is true or not.

In those days, the Crows didn't consider it wrong for a brave to have more than one wife at a time. In fact, because so many braves were killed fighting other tribes, there was a shortage of men to marry, so, if a warrior had several wives, that was fine with everybody.

In 1802, President Thomas Jefferson made the Louisiana Purchase in which the U.S. government bought from France much of the land considered by the plains tribes to belong to them. You know, Indians didn't own specific parcels of land; the land occupied by each tribe belonged to the whole tribe and not to individual members of the tribe. There were also no boundary lines between what one tribe considered its territory and what its neighbors considered theirs. Well, as you can imagine, neighboring tribes went to war with each other over disputed territorial boundaries. This kind of dispute has occurred thousands of times over many centuries in loads of places around the world.

The plains tribes didn't accept the Louisiana Purchase. They considered themselves separate nations. They didn't pay any attention to the laws of the United States. And, during the time that Jim lived with the Crows, the United States didn't try to enforce its laws on the Indian nations. Even though Jim was a U.S. citizen, the one-wife-at-a-time rule that the U.S. government followed was not applied to him during his tribal years.

Who were all Jim's Crow wives, and how did each of them like having to compete with one another? Didn't jealousies among them cause big problems? Nope. Jealousy among Indians was almost unknown—among women and men. If one brave was particularly successful in battle, the other warriors weren't envious—they were truly happy for the fellow who had done better than they. (Wouldn't it be nice if we all could be like that instead of envying someone who is more successful?)

Of Jim's six original wives, the only one I could find out about was his first. When Jim joined the Crows he was allowed to choose one of three sisters for a wife. He chose Still-water, the oldest. In Jim's book he states: "She was affectionate, obedient, gentle, cheerful and apparently quite happy—even in later years when I took additional squaws for wives."

Among wives two through six were two women who were from the Blackfoot tribe, the tribe with whom the Crows fought more than any other. Although it may seem strange for a Crow man to take an enemy woman for a wife, it was done all the

Sue Beckwourth, a Crow Indian, was Jim's last wife. (I've never found a picutre of any of the others.) She lived with him at Pueblo, Colorado, when he helped establish the town and at his ranch on the edge of Beckwourth Valley in the Sierra mountains of California. (Painted in 1998 by Hilliar Moore; courtesy of the Beckwourth Cabin Museum, Beckwourth, CA.)

time. When in battle, Indians killed only the opposing men. The women and children were made captives and brought back to live with the Crows. Jim's book explains that the Crow men treated all women better than the Blackfoot men did. (I'll bet the Blackfoot men said that they were nicer than the Crows.) The prisoners quickly blended into their new tribe and were accepted as if they'd never been part of an enemy tribe.

One day, after Jim already had six Crow wives, a little girl only 13 or 14 years old came up to him and said she also wanted to be his wife. Jim turned her away saying, correctly, that she was much too young. Disregarding his rejection, she kept after him. So, a year or two later he finally gave in and married her.

However, Jim insisted that for the next several years she was to remain a virgin until she got older. Jim always fondly referred to her as "Little Wife." Eventually she gave birth to the only child Jim mentions from the time he lived with the Crows. This son was named Black Panther (no connection with 20th-century Black Panthers), and his nickname was Little Jim. He was loved by the whole tribe and was raised by his grandfather when Jim left the Crows. In his book, Jim never discusses Little Jim beyond childhood except to mention that, by 1855, Black Panther had become first counselor (a rank just below the top chief) of the Crow nation.

Jim's next Crow wife, Pine Leaf, was an unusual person. Crow women didn't go to war, but she did—and was fiercer than many male warriors. Evidently Jim really admired her and asked her on many occasions to marry him. For years she refused and continued to excel at warring, but she didn't marry anyone else. At long last she retired from fighting and agreed to be Jim's wife, I calculated that she was wife number eight. But, in typical Jim Beckwourth style, not long after their wedding he took off and never spent much time with Pine Leaf again nor with Little Wife or any of the others.

After he left the Crows for the last time, he had three more marriages. In those days, no one thought he had to divorce his many Crow wives before getting married again. Jim's next wife was Senorita Luisa Sandoval (when converted from Spanish to English, her name became Louise Sanderville). They lived for several years near the town that he helped found, Pueblo, Colorado, and they had a daughter named Matilda.

As usual, Jim left this little family when he went to live in California for several years. When he returned, he found that Luisa had married a man by the name of John Brown, even

Town of Beckwourth, California on the edge of Sierra Valley (which was originally called Beckwourth Valley). The town is a few miles from Jim's old ranch and trading post. California State Highway 70 runs through the middle of town. (Photo by Woodward Payne.)

though she and Jim hadn't been divorced. Evidently this Brown guy had come back from California before Jim did and had a forged (fake) letter to her from Jim saying that Jim didn't want to be married to her anymore. Brown asked her to marry him, and, thinking that she'd been rejected by Jim, she agreed. Jim showed up several months later, and poor Luisa was shocked to find that her former husband hadn't written that letter. She offered to leave Brown-the-forger and rejoin Jim. But Jim just said "Never you mind" and moved on, leaving his daughter, Matilda, to be raised by Luisa and Brown. The Browns later moved to San Bernardino, California, and raised nine more children.

His next wife was Elizabeth Lettbetter from Denver, whom he married in a formal and legal wedding ceremony (for a change). They had two children, a son, George, and a daughter, Julia, who died when she was less than two years old. Julia's death was evidently a real blow to the family, and the marriage broke up a year later. Jim left George to be raised by Elizabeth, and George died at about age 12 when he was kicked by a mule.

Well, that might have been the end of Jim's married life, but was it? Nope. Along came Sue, another Crow Indian, to become wife number eleven. Jim stayed with Sue for longer than any of his previous wives. The couple didn't live with the tribe but instead on a farm south of Denver, near the South Platte River. Entertaining Indians was one of their pleasures, and often a dozen tepees would be set up around the Beckwourth farmhouse.

Several years later, after Jim had completed his famous emigrant trail (read about it in Chapter 19), he and Sue moved to California. They built a cabin and ranch on the western edge of a large valley that became known as Beckwourth Valley, but was later renamed Sierra Valley, near where the tiny town of Beckwourth is now located. Here, too, Indians from various tribes came to visit, setting up their tepees nearby and enjoying a welcome from Jim and Sue.

Jim and Sue occasionally traveled to San Francisco. They would go to the theater attended by some of San Francisco's prominent citizens. It's nice to note that black Jim and his Crow wife felt at ease associating with San Francisco's white society.

Have you been wondering about Jim's lack of commitment to and affection for his children? We know that Black Panther (Little Jim) reached adulthood, but no life history of him is available, so we don't know whether he had children of his own. Matilda, his daughter with Luisa, grew up in San Bernardino, evidently married, and had at least one daughter. I've never been able to find out anything more about this one known granddaughter of Jim's.

18

Racism in the Old Wild West

During the first half of the 1800s, when the West was still wild, were the white trappers, mountain men, and early pioneers prejudiced against blacks? Although Jim was bi-racial, he would have been considered a black man. Well, it doesn't appear that he experienced racism, based on the research I've done.

Nowhere in Jim's book does he mention feeling that the white men he associated with were prejudiced against him because of his color. Now, that doesn't prove that there was no racism against blacks. It might be that Jim merely decided not to mention it in his book. So, to check this out, let's look at what other people who knew Jim had to say on the subject.

Most had nothing but good things to say about him, and later books about Jim's life don't discuss racism. There were only two exceptions.

A guy named Francis Parkman wrote about Jim with clear anti-black feelings, describing Jim as a bad person. Now, Parkman first visited the West several years after Jim had died, so Parkman never actually knew Jim. Other writers didn't describe Jim as a bad person. In fact, most people who knew Jim praised him as honest, brave, friendly, outgoing, eager for fun, and a good friend to many. So, I've concluded that this guy Parkman was prejudiced against blacks and Jim in particular, although he knew about Jim only from secondhand information. A pair of other writers, Frank Triplett and Charles Christy, also demonstrated their prejudice against blacks in writing about Jim (their writings have been thoroughly discredited). Because of these examples, I can't say that there was absolutely no racism by whites against blacks in the old Wild West, but the prejudiced guys were certainly few in number.

Most writers talking about relationships among the early trappers and mountain men point out that these men judged

The domed "beehive" oven at the Taos, New Mexico, pueblo was used by the Indian women for baking bread. In the 1840s, Mexicans murdered all the Americans living in Taos. Jim became prejudiced against Mexicans because of these murders, and in 1847 he joined U.S. army troops to fight them in the Mexican-American War.

one another as individuals and by their accomplishments, not by the color of their skin. The few blacks who were among the first travelers to the plains and Rocky Mountains (yes, there were some other than Jim) suffered the same hardships and faced the same dangers as their white companions. They were respected for their ability to overcome all the tough situations they ran into.

Among the few other black men in the old Wild West during the first half of the 1800s, one of the most famous was a fellow called York, the only nonwhite man to accompany Lewis and Clark on their great three-year exploration of the unknown lands between St. Louis and the Pacific Ocean. York was a slave owned by Clark. (Did you know that commonly slaves weren't given family names? It's true, so his whole name was merely York.) In the reading I've done about Lewis and Clark's journey, there's no mention of any prejudice against York.

Another well-known free multi-racial black man in the early West was a fellow by the name of Edward Rose. Ed was one of the first group of trappers ever to travel from St. Louis to the Rocky Mountains, even before Jim did so. Ed went to live with the Crows, too, several years before Jim did, and he probably made it easier for Jim to be accepted by the tribe. Ed was known as one of the best interpreters ever known in all of Indian country (as Jim was a few years later), having learned several native languages. Ed lived with the Crows off and on all of his life, so it's most likely that he and Jim knew one another (although Jim doesn't mention Ed in his book). Aside from his skill as an interpreter, Ed didn't have a great reputation. One day, in a fight, his opponent bit the tip of Ed's nose off. Ed's life came to a sad ending when some unfriendly Indians of another tribe were about to capture him. Rather than be

Fort Vasquez, 53 miles north of Denver next to the town of Platteville, Colorado. In 1835 Jim was put in charge of the fort by his good buddy Louis Vasquez.

captured and tortured by these Indians, Ed decided he'd kill himself first. He stood next to a whole barrel of gunpowder and exploded it.

Although whites didn't seem to show much racism against blacks in the old Wild West, they were certainly racist against Indians and Mexicans. The bigotry against Indians came about partly because the whites feared the Indians. As we know, fear causes racism. Much has been written about Indians' savagery against white emigrants, but the opposite is also true. After all, the Indians were merely trying to protect their lands and their culture.

Whites' hatred of Mexicans in the old Wild West grew over a period of time. The Mexicans came first to parts of what are today Texas, New Mexico, Colorado, Arizona, and California. Naturally they objected when white explorers and settlers came into the territory that they already occupied.

How about Jim—was he a prejudiced person? Certainly he had no problem with white people. He was clearly very fond of his father; throughout his life just about all of his best buddies were white; and his book never mentions any grudge against white people. Nor was Jim racist against Indians. The proof is the many years he lived with the Crows, his good relationships with other tribes, and his marriage to Sue, a Crow woman, toward the end of his lifetime.

Was Jim a bigot against Mexicans? Well, one of his wives, Luisa Sandoval, was supposedly of Mexican descent. And the cousins Louis and Pike Vasquez were friends (and business partners) of Jim's, although they have Mexican names. But Jim did admit in his book, "I had felt no great liking for them [Mexicans] since the awful tragedy at Taos" (Mexicans had murdered all the white people living in the town of Taos, which is now a popular New Mexico tourist spot).

Later in his life, Jim joined the white Californians who were fighting the armed forces of the Mexican Republic in California. So, I can't say that Jim was completely without prejudice against anybody. But it seems that his anti-Mexican feelings were created by wars, and wars can make almost anyone dislike the people on the opposing side.

19

Jim Builds a Famous Trail

The discovery of gold in California in 1848 brought thousands of men during the next several years to search for gold. Prospectors (men who went looking for new areas where gold could be found) combed the mountains of northern California trying to discover another mother lode (a huge amount of mineable gold).

In the spring of 1850, 50-year-old Jim was prospecting with a friend in the northern part of California's Sierra mountains in a big valley that hadn't been explored before. To his surprise he saw a pass over the mountains that seemed lower than any of the other passes then being used by emigrants rushing to California in covered wagons. A lower pass would mean that the tired horses and oxen pulling the wagons wouldn't have to struggle uphill as far to get over the Sierra. Also, a lower pass would mean less snow if the wagons hadn't crossed the mountains before winter started.

Jim's cabin store near the Middle Fork of the Feather River in California. Pioneers in their covered wagons traveling on the Beckwourth Emigrant Trail stopped here for supplies on their way farther into California. Several years ago this building was moved a couple of miles from its original site on Jim's old ranch to where it stands today on the edge of Beckwourth (Sierra) Valley.

The emigrants all knew of the tragic experience of the Donner Party. That group crossed the Sierra too late and got snowed in. Unable to go farther, they camped in the snow, and, as food ran out, members of the group starved to death. Some of them finally got across the mountains to safety and told how their friends had suffered horrible deaths due to starvation. These tales caused great concern among new emigrants as they approached the mountains in their covered wagons.

Jim didn't say anything to his buddy about his discovery of this pass. He kept his knowledge secret, resolving to return later to explore the pass some more. When he did, he decided that he could build a trail over the pass. It would go over the Sierra mountains and end in the town of Marysville in the Sacramento River Valley 41 miles north of Sacramento.

Jim went to the mayor of Marysville and explained his idea for a trail. He pointed out to the mayor that the merchants in Sacramento were all getting rich because Sacramento was the end of the California Trail (the route the Donner Party had used) and so was where the emigrants bought supplies. There was no place to buy anything between Salt Lake City, Utah, and Sacramento, California, a journey that took more than a month.

The mayor readily understood that if Jim's trail ended in Marysville, the merchants there would get rich, so he welcomed Jim's plan. He agreed to raise over $6,000 from the town's soon-to-be-rich store owners to pay Jim. But when Jim asked for some of the money to pay his costs for building the wagon road, the mayor said, "I'll pay you when it's completed, not before."

Well, Jim just went ahead creating his new trail, paying all the expenses out of his own pocket. He hired a crew of three guys, and they worked building the wagon road during the summer and fall of 1850 and the spring and summer of 1851. Jim's road headed northwest where the main California Trail turned south, at the junction of Steamboat Creek and the Truckee River, now the site of Sparks, Nevada. The western end of the road was at Bidwell's Bar, which is now under the lake created by Oroville Dam, where there already was a wagon and stagecoach road running from the local mining camps to Marysville.

At last the trail was completed in late August, and Jim proudly led the very first group of emigrants and their covered wagons over his route across the Sierra mountains at the pass he'd discovered. To everyone's delight, this first group of wagons arrived in Marysville on August 30, 1851. The town celebrated (I'm sure the poor and tired travelers did, too). However, the next day, before Jim could meet with the mayor to claim his payment, the town caught fire, and almost all of it burned to the ground. In those days, most stores and houses were built only of wood and burned easily. Because fire engines hadn't been invented yet, when a fire started in a town it would usually burn many buildings—there were no well-trained firemen or good firefighting equipment to put it out.

The town's shop owners surveyed their burned stores, which had contained all their goods for sale. The mayor told Jim the bad news that there was no money to pay him. The mayor had intended to get the payment money from the merchants, who would have benefited from the new wagon road. But now they'd have to use all their cash to rebuild and restock their stores.

Even when the merchants finally rebuilt and got rich, because more emigrants flocked to Marysville over Jim's trail, he never received the payment he'd earned.

Beckwourth Pass looking toward the west. Jim's trail went over this pass, which was the lowest emigrant pass across the Sierra mountains. Today, California State Highway 70 passes over the pass and the Union Pacific Railroad tracks cross under the pass in a tunnel. (Photo by Woodward Payne.)

The only financial benefit he got from all his trail building work came in an unexpected way. Tired from the huge effort, he established a ranch about 20 miles west of the famous pass he'd discovered. He chose a beautiful valley (once called Beckwourth Valley but now called Sierra Valley—and it's still beautiful). Here he settled down with his Indian wife, Sue, and built a small hotel and trading post. His book states:

> I finally found myself transformed into a hotel-keeper and chief of a trading-post. My house is considered the emigrant's landing-place, as it is the first ranch he arrives at in the golden state [California] and is the only house between this point and Salt Lake [Utah]. Here is a valley 240 miles in circumference containing some of the choicest land in the world . . . . When I stand at my door and watch the weary, way-worn travelers approach, their wagons holding together by a miracle, their stock [horses, cows, and oxen] in the last stage of emaciation [starvation] and themselves a ragged bunch, I frequently amuse myself with imagining the contrast between how they now look and how they must have looked to their admiring friends when they first set out upon their journey.

One traveler who paused at Jim's place later wrote: "His nature was a hospitable and generous one, and he supplied the pressing necessities of starving emigrants, often without money—they agreeing to pay him later, which I regret to say, a number of them failed to do. This so impoverished him that

Wagon wheel tracks on the Beckwourth Emigrant Trail. At this spot the trail is near Big Grizzly Creek, which was named after a big bear who often threatened the passing emigrants.

he was compelled to give up his place and resume a wandering life."

Still, Jim evidently did make *some* money there, because his book says that running his hotel and trading post was his only benefit for having built the trail.

People passing Jim's ranch would often mention that tepees were set up nearby. Evidently Indians who weren't Crows knew of Jim's success as a Crow chief. He was loved and respected, so tribes felt comfortable locating for a short time nearby the famous former Crow chief. The fact that Jim's Crow wife, Sue, lived with him at the ranch probably made the visiting Indians feel even more welcome.

Of the 75,000 people traveling west each year during that era, Jim estimated that the majority would use his wagon road. Although his pass attracted a good number of emigrants, it never became as popular as he had originally expected. For example, in 1855 approximately 10,150 settlers used his trail, but many groups chose Noble's Road, the Carson Route, or the Truckee branch of the California Trail, now called the Donner Trail.

A stop at Jim's ranch did save dozens of wagon trains that might never have reached the Sacramento River Valley because they were in such poor shape once they had crossed the Sierra.

After 1858, use of his route diminished because other wagon roads over the Sierra had been improved, making them easier than Jim's trail. Then, in 1868, the first railroad across the nation was completed. After that, pioneer wagon roads went unused, because it was a lot easier to get to California by railroad than by covered wagon. Years later, in 1908, the second railroad line built across the Sierra mountains into California used the pass that Jim had discovered.

Today, Jim's trail lives on in history and is known as the Beckwourth Emigrant Trail. Most of the route has been identified by an organization called Trails West whose members have placed markers along the way. The markers are made of steel railroad

One of the signs placed about every two miles along the route of the Beckwourth Emigrant Trail. These markers are made of railroad rails and were erected by the group Trails West, Inc., in the early 1990s.

rails, cut and welded to form a T, and each marker weighs 200 pounds. Attached to the upper portion of the T is an inscribed plate bearing a description of that particular place along the trail. The descriptions are taken from writings by pioneers who camped at or passed by that spot in the 1850s. The tracks of wagons from over 150 years ago can still be seen in a few places if you hike along the route of Jim's famous trail, now long gone. I've spent many hours hiking along that route.

Jim's name is preserved today in several ways in the area. The pass over the Sierra mountains that he discovered is called Beckwourth Pass. At an altitude of 5,212 feet, it is 2,000 feet lower than Donner Pass, the popular emigrant route to Sacramento.

On the northwestern edge of Sierra Valley is a small community named Beckwourth. The town went through the same change in spelling its name that Jim did. Until 1921, the town was named Beckwith; then it changed to Beckwourth. Even today, the Beckwith Tavern is located in Beckwourth. Are you confused yet?

One of the highest mountain peaks in the region near the town of Beckwourth is named Beckwourth Peak. On its summit are a bunch of microwave and cell phone towers that allow modern communications to pass through the area, a helpful (but ugly) use of Beckwourth Peak.

If Jim were alive today he'd be mighty surprised to see all this modern stuff on "his" peak and all the developments near his once-remote ranch.

20

The Mystery of Jim's Death

Jim died when he was 66 years old (or 68, if he really was born in 1798, as his book says). In those days if a person lived to 66, that was well beyond the average lifespan for men in the United States. The super health that Jim had enjoyed most of his life was fading by the time he was 66. He still stood straight and tall, but he'd been bothered by rheumatism (a word that isn't much used by doctors anymore because it's now called arthritis, a painful swelling and stiffness of the joints and muscles). Considering the number of nights Jim had slept on the cold, hard ground with only a blanket, it's a wonder he could move around at all.

There are several versions of how Jim died and it remains a mystery. Storytellers dreamed up tales of how it happened, but there was no conclusive evidence of the truth. I'll tell you the version I like best, although it may not be true—but no one can say for sure.

The most commonly shown photo of Jim. It must have been taken late in his life, because his face shows the wear of all his travels and adventures. (Courtesy of the Nevada Historical Society.)

Before 1866, most tribes fought the white men in defense of their lands. However, the Crow nation was hesitant to do so, because, many years before, Jim had taught them to be friends with the white men, even though the settlers were taking over Indian land.

Colonel Henry Carrington of the U.S. army wished to continue at peace with the Crows, so he asked three famous old mountain men to go meet with the tribe on a peace mission. One of the men was Jim, because he spoke their language and was respected by the Crows.

Jim hadn't visited the Crows in 29 years. He must have felt sad as he went on this important visit, because he was no longer returning to the tribe as the triumphant Chief Medicine Calf. He also knew that the Crows would have to sign the treaty in humiliation, or else they'd be wiped out by the American soldiers.

When the Crows saw Jim, they rejoiced, thinking that their heroic Medicine Calf was returning to be their chief one last time. Imagine their disappointment when they discovered that he had come for just a short visit to talk them into a peace treaty.

Yes, the Crows listened to Jim saying that peace was in the best interest of the tribe, and they reluctantly agreed to do what Jim asked. Upon conclusion of the peace treaty, the other two mountain men left immediately. Jim stayed behind for the evening, when the Crows honored him with a good-bye ceremony.

At the celebration, Jim, the guest of honor, was fed a bowl of delicious meat. But when he ate it, he became sick and died. The Crows had poisoned the meat and killed him.

Why would they do that? History tells us that Jim was their favorite

Painting of Jim by Hilliar Moore, who must have used the black-and-white photo of Jim (in this chapter) as his model. Mr. Moore certainly didn't try to make Jim seem more cheerful than he is in the photo. (Courtesy of the Beckwourth Cabin Museum, Beckwourth, CA.)

When this Denver church was founded in 1882 it was named Beckwourth Methodist/Episcopal Church because it was on Beckwourth Street. Many years ago some town committee got the dumb idea of renaming a bunch of streets that had been named after important people. Beckwourth Street became West 5th Avenue (boring!).

chief—he had made the Crows the strongest tribe in the region. When asked, the Crows explained that they wanted their great warrior to remain with them forever, and in death he would do so. "He had been our good medicine [good luck]," they said. "If we could not have him living with us, it would be good to have him dead so his spirit and 'good medicine' remains with us forever. His bones must remain with us for the protection of his people."

The tribe buried Jim in a secret grave and never told anyone where it was. No one has ever known where he was laid to rest except the Indians who attended Jim's burial ceremony.

Jim's favorite Crow wife, Pine Leaf, and his son, Black Panther, might have been living with the Crows at the time of the poisoning; it was known that they weren't living with Jim or among the white settlers. Did his wife and son know of the plans to poison him? Were they at the good-bye celebration? We'll never know.

Is that really the way he died? The Crows admitted that they had poisoned him. However, another version of the story leaves out the peace treaty and just says that the Crows had invited him back for a celebration.

Others believe that he wasn't poisoned at all, that instead he'd been sick at the time of this last visit to the Crows and just died of his illness while he was there.

All versions of the story agree on one thing: Jim was with the Crows when he died and was secretly buried by them in a location that was never revealed.

And so ends the story of James Pearson Beckwourth, born a bi-racial slave, who became one of the greatest Indian chiefs, and one of the all-time best mountain men, a saver of lives, a great traveler, and a many-skilled job-hopper, in the earliest days of the American West.

APPENDIX 1

How Mountain Men Trapped Beavers

Trapping beavers was the main occupation of mountain men. So, I thought you might like to know how they did it.

First, they'd find a place along a mountain stream that looked like a good spot for beavers to live. One clue was a dam built by beavers across the stream. Another was a tree stump

Rusty beaver trap given to me by a neighbor, Bob Danner, who found it in the forest several miles from the site of Jim's old cabin in the Sierra mountains.

or bush that showed beaver tooth marks. Beavers have sharp front teeth that they use to chew into the base of a tree. With enough chewing they can cut down trees as big as you can wrap your hands around.

The beavers drag the downed trees to the water and place them across the creek. Yes, those cute little animals can do enormous amounts of work. They then fill in the dam with branches, small rocks, and mud. I've seen several of these amazing dams on the Middle Fork of the Feather River only a few miles from where Jim's cabin was located. A large pond forms behind the dam, and the beavers live there.

Now, the beavers could smell where the trapper had walked, and this would scare them away. But the trapper fooled them by wading in the cold water from a distance upstream. When he had waded to where the beaver family lived, he'd find a level spot on the bottom of the stream. There he'd set down a steel trap and stand on the jaws of the trap to lock it open. When the jaws were spread apart, the trapper placed bait on the trap. Then he stuck a pole firmly into the bottom of the stream near the trap. A ring was attached to the trap by a chain, and the trapper slipped the ring over the pole to hold the trap in place.

The beaver was attracted by the smell of the bait, even though it was under water. The unsuspecting critter would check out the smell and step on the trap. Wham! The trap jaws would snap shut around the beaver's foot or leg. The poor beaver would struggle to get free, but the ring held the trap fast, so the beaver couldn't swim away with it.

What happened next is pretty gross, I know. Occasionally the beaver did pull its foot and leg free, but it always suffered severe injury. Sometimes it would even chew its own foot off

A beaver went to all the trouble of chewing down these two small trees but for some reason never bothered to drag them down to the Middle Fork of the Feather River only about half a block away. Jim's ranch was about a mile from where this beaver was building its dam, so it's possible that Jim once upon a time trapped beavers near this spot.

to get free. Most of the time the beaver couldn't pull free. Now, a beaver swimming under water needs to pop up to the surface every couple of minutes to get a breath of air. Perhaps you can guess what happened. Because the trapped animal couldn't reach the surface of the creek for some air, it quickly drowned.

Well, the trapper's job was to kill the animal one way or another, so any way he did it would have been cruel. However, purposely drowning the cute furry beaver seems particularly awful to me. Thank goodness most beaver trapping stopped over 100 years ago.

APPENDIX 2

Timeline of Jim's Adventures

(Pinning exact dates to Jim's adventures is not possible because a lot of information is missing or conflicting—but here are the best dates I can come up with.)

1800	Jim is born in Frederick County, Virginia. (Jim's book says that he was born in 1798 in Fredericksburg, Virginia, but many historians claim that the correct year and place are 1800 and Frederick County. All subsequent dates in this list assume 1800 to be when he was born.)
1801–1807	Jim is raised as a slave on his dad's plantation.
1807–08	His dad moves the family to St. Louis with Jim and several other slaves. (There are no records showing just when the Beckwiths moved. All public records mentioning Jim's father in Frederick County end in 1801, and no records appear elsewhere until 1809 court records in St. Charles, Missouri.)

1810	His dad moves the family and slaves to The Point; Jim is sent to school in St. Louis.
1814	Jim ends his schooling, and begins working as a blacksmith for George Casner in St. Louis.
1819	He's fired by Casner.
1819–1822	No records show where Jim was during these years.
1822	Goes to the lead mines in Fever River (now Galena), Illinois.
1823	Returns to St. Louis from Fever River. Travels by steamboat from St. Louis to New Orleans, falls ill with yellow fever, and returns to St. Louis after ten days.
1824	Joins General Ashley's second ill-fated expedition

Historic marker mounted on a large stone at the top of Beckwourth Pass on California State Highway 70. For many modern-day travelers who stop to read it, this may be their first introduction to who Jim Beckwourth was.

to the Wild West, with a man named Moses Harris (nicknamed "Black" Harris because of his wild black hair and beard). Jim leaves General Ashley and walks 300 miles to Curtis and Eley's trading post at the mouth of the Kansas River. Works at a trading post on the Missouri River. Returns to St. Louis. Jim's father appears in court to free Jim from slavery (also in 1825 and 1826). Jim travels with another Ashley expedition to the Rockies. Returns to St. Louis. Leaves for the West again in November with General Ashley.

1825   Participates in the first Mountain Fair Rendezvous on the Green River. Returns to St. Louis with General Ashley. Leaves for the mountains in the autumn with Jedediah Smith.

1826–27   Works as a free trapper in the Rocky Mountains.

1828   Goes on his fourth trapping expedition. Attends the 1828 Rendezvous at the south end of Bear Lake in northern Utah. Joins the Crow Indian tribe.

1829–35   Lives with the Crows. Becomes chief of the Crows in about 1833.

1835   Leaves the Crows. Is put in charge of Fort Vasquez (now Plattsville, Colorado), by Louis Vasquez.

1836   Is a trapper for American Fur Company. Rejoins the Crows, but soon leaves for St. Louis.

1837   Visits the Crows for a short time. Returns to St. Louis because he no longer can supply the fur company he works for with furs.

1837   Forms a group of mountain men in St. Louis to go to Florida to fight in the Seminole War. Goes to Florida as an express rider.

Here's what Denver looked like in 1860, shortly after the town was founded. Jim's store is the small building third from the right with the white front and the two large upper windows. It was on Ferry Street between Larimer and Market Streets. Now how, you may ask, did I get an aerial photo of old Denver 45 years before the Wright brothers invented the airplane? Well, this is actually a photo of a very detailed model of the 1860 town, which I found at the Colorado History Museum. (Courtesy of the Colorado Historical Society.)

1838	Returns to St. Louis from Florida. Is hired by William Sublette as a trader in the southern plains.
1839	Works for Sublette as a trader.
1840–41	Establishes trading posts in Colorado for the Bent brothers.

1842	Establishes his own store in Taos, New Mexico. Marries Luisa Sandoval. Moves to the Arkansas River, and with several other men establishes a fort trading post called the Pueblo.
1843	Others move to Pueblo, and it becomes a town. Jim's daughter Matilda is born.
1844	Travels to California, and establishes a trading post at Pueblo de los Angeles. Becomes one of the first 100 non-Mexican, non-Indian residents of Los Angeles. Moves to Soda Springs, but soon leaves to travel in the Sierra mountains.
1845	Is involved in the Bear Flag Rebellion of Californians fighting the Mexicans.
1846	Returns to Pueblo. Acts as a dispatch carrier for the U.S. army to and from Santa Fe, New Mexico. Moves to Denver, and opens a hotel with a partner.
1847	Joins U.S. forces in the battle to defeat the Mexicans at Taos, New Mexico. Carries dispatches for the army.
1848	Continues as a guide, interpreter, and dispatch carrier throughout the Southwest and Kansas.
1848	Leaves Santa Fe for California. Goes to Monterey, California, and works as a dispatch rider. Carries mail to many places between San Diego and San Francisco.
1849	Takes a steamship to Stockton, California, with clothing for sale. Establishes a store in Stockton in a tent. Moves from Stockton to Sonora. Sells the Sonora store to a partner, and goes to Sacramento. Returns to Santa Fe from Sacramento.

Site of Jim's Denver farm, which he bought in 1863. If he were alive today he'd be mighty surprised to see all those modern office buildings so close to his property. Two baseball fields and a large pond are part of a city park now located on the site.

1850   Comes back to the Sierra mountains of California to take part in the gold rush.

1850–51   Hires three men to help him build an emigrant trail across the Sierra mountains.

1851   Leads the first wagon train of emigrants over his trail to Marysville.

1852   Establishes a ranch and trading post near the trail on the edge of Beckwourth Valley.

1853–54   Operates the trading post and does ranching.

1854–55   Dictates his life story to Thomas Bonner.

1856   Jim's and Bonner's book on Jim's life is published.

1858   Leaves California for a final time, and returns to Kansas City, Missouri.

1859	Moves from Kansas City to Denver. Is employed by A. Pike Vasquez as a merchant in Denver.
1860	Gets a job as the local Indian agent in Denver. Continues to run the Denver store for Vasquez. Leaves Vasquez, and establishes his own ranch in South Denver. Marries Elizabeth Lettbetter.
1861	Continues being a rancher.
1862	Leaves ranching, and acts as a guide for the U.S. army. Runs a farm owned by A. Pike Vasquez.
1863–64	Buys and runs his own farm.
1864	Acts as a guide for the U.S. army again. Is a witness to the Sand Creek massacre of Cheyenne Indians by the U.S. army.
1865–66	Works as a dispatch rider out of Fort Laramie, Wyoming.
1866	Moves back to Denver. Joins Jim Bridger as a trader with the Indians. Goes back to the Crows to make a treaty for the U.S. government. Dies while visiting the Crows.

Bibliography

Books and Other Sources I Checked to Learn about Jim

Books

Alter, J. Cecil. *Jim Bridger.* 1925.

Bacon, Melvin, and Daniel Blegen. *Crossroads of Cultures on the Santa Fe Trail.* 1995.

Bancroft, Hubert Howe. *Chronicles of Builders of Commonwealth.* 1851.

Beckwith, Paul. *The Beckwiths.* 1891.

Bonner, T. D. *The Life and Adventures of James P. Beckwourth.* [Autobiography as dictated to Bonner by Jim.] Introduction and commentary by Delmont R. Oswald. 1972.

Bonner, T. D. *The Life and Adventures of James P. Beckwourth.* [Autobiography as dictated to Bonner by Jim.] Introduction by Bernard DeVoto. 1931.

Caughey, John W. *California.* 1940.

Cortesi, Lawrence. *Jim Beckwourth: Explorer—Patriot of the Rockies.* 1971.

Dolan, Sean. *James Beckwourth: Frontiersman.* 1972.

Fariss and Smith [no first names listed]. *The History of Plumas County.* 1882.

Felton, Harold W. *Jim Beckwourth: Negro Mountain Man.* 1966.

Glass, Andrew. *Mountain Men: True Grit and Tall Tales.* 2000.

Goodstein, Phil. *Denver Streets: Names, Numbers, Locations, Logic.* 1994.

Gowans, Fred R. *Rocky Mountain Rendezvous: A History of the Fur Trade Rendezvous 1825–1840.* 2005.

Hall, Frank. *History of the State of Colorado.* 1889.

Hammond, Andrew, and Joanne Hammond. *Following the Beckwourth Trail.* 1994.

Howard, Frederick Thomas. *First Roads to California.* 1998.

Hunt, Thomas. *Ghost Trails to California.* 1974.

Katz, William Loren. *The Black West.* 1971, 1987.

Lavender, David. *Bent's Fort.* 1954.

Lecompte, Janet. *Pueblo, Hardscrabble, Greenhorn: Society on the High Plains, 1832–1856.* 1978.

Locke, Raymond Friday. *James Beckwourth, Mountain Man. Black American Series.* 1995.

Manheimer, Ann S. *James Beckwourth: Legendary Mountain Man.* 2006.

Meyers, Laurie. *Lewis and Clark and Me: A Dog's Tale.* 2002.

Morgan, Dale. *The West of William Ashley.* 1964.

Mumey, Nolie. *James Pierson Beckwourth 1856–1866.* 1957.

Place, Marian T. *Mountain Man: The Life of Jim Beckwourth.* 1970.

Reef, Catherine. *Black Explorers.* 1996.

Shephard, Betty, and James B. Shephard. *The Life of Jim Beckwourth.* 1968.

Smiley, Jerome C. *History of Denver.* 1901.

Stewart, George R. *The California Trail.* 1962.

Stone, Wilbur Fisk. *History of Colorado.* 1918.

Wilson, Elinor. *Jim Beckwourth: Black Mountain Man and War Chief of the Crows.* 1972.

Pamphlets and Articles

Bailey, Stanley. *James P. Beckwourth.* Plumas County Historical Society Publication no. 13, no date.

"Captain James Beckwourth." *Rocky Mountain News,* 1860.

Early History of Lead Region of Wisconsin. Wisconsin Historical Collections, vol. 6, 1872.

The Galena Gazette, Galena, IL, July 20, 1988.

A General History of Sierra Valley. Plumas County Historical Society Publication no. 2, December 4, 1960.

Hafen, LeRoy R. "The Last Years of James P. Beckwourth." *The Colorado Magazine,* vol. 4, no. 4, August 1928.

Hammond, Andrew. *The Remarkable James Beckwourth,* no date.

Hammond, Andrew, and Joanne Hammond. "Mapping the Beckwourth Trail." *Overland Journal,* fall 1994.

History of the Beckwourth Trail. Plumas Corporation and Oregon-California Trails Association, no date.

Morgan, Charles. "Huckster on Horseback." *Westways,* November 1968.

News from the Plains, January 1996.

"The North American Beaver Trade." *Cobbleston History Magazine for Young People,* June 1982.

Rogers, James Grafton. "Colorado Mountain Men." *The Colorado Magazine,* vol. 30, no. 3, January 1953.

Historical Societies, Libraries, Museums, and Other Places

African-American Heritage Tour from Winchester Visitors' Bureau, Winchester, VA.

Beckwourth Cabin Museum, Beckwourth, CA.

Bent's Old Fort National Historic Site, La Junta, CO.

Colorado History Museum and Stephen H. Hart Research Library, Denver.

Colorado's Newspaper Historic Collection, Denver.

Confluence Point Missouri State Park, West Alton, MO.

El Pueblo History Museum, Pueblo, CO.

Fort Laramie National Historic Site, Fort Laramie, WY.

Fort Union National Monument, Fort Union, NM.

Fort Vasquez Museum, Platteville, CO.

Galena Historical Society and Library, Galena, IL.

Galena/Jo Daviess County Historical Museum, Galena, IL.

Handley Regional Library, Stewart Bell Archives, Winchester, VA.

Independence Rock State Historic Site, Casper, WY.

Ladede's Landing, St. Louis.

Little Big Horn Battlefield Historical Museum and National Monument,
     Hardin, MT.

Los Angeles Public Library, History Department, Los Angeles.

Museum of Indian Art, Santa Fe, NM.

Museum of Westward Expansion, St. Louis.

Nevada Historical Society, Reno, NV.

Oregon Trail Ruts State Historic Site, Guernsey, WY.

Plains Indian Museum, part of the Buffalo Bill Historical Center, Cody, WY.

Plumas County Library, Portola Branch, Portola, CA.

Plumas County Library, Quincy Branch, Quincy, CA.

Plumas County Museum, Quincy, CA.

Rendezvous 1829 site, Landers, WY.

Rendezvous 1838 Historic Site, Riverton, WY.

Richmond County Museum, Warsaw, VA.

South Pass State Historic Site, South Pass City, WY.

St. Louis Public Library, Archives and History, St. Louis.

Taos Pueblo, Taos, NM.

Winchester/Frederick Historical Society, Winchester, VA.

Wind River Indian Reservation, Fort Washakie, WY.

Index

Note: In the following index, the initials "JB" refer to Jim Beckwourth; page numbers in *italics* refer to illustrations and their captions.

About Me, the Author

People ask me all the time, "How'd you ever hear of Jim Beckwourth?" Well, I'm the author of an award-winning hiking book, *Feather River Country Adventure Trails*. It describes 101 hikes in the Sierra mountains of California. Jim's ranch

Me standing on the front porch of Jim's old trading post located near the route of his emigrant trail.

(the one I tell about in Chapter 19) was on the Middle Fork of the Feather River, near where the river starts. Four of the hikes in my book follow portions of the Beckwourth Emigrant Trail, the wagon road Jim built across the Sierra mountains in 1850 and 1851. I've spent lots of enjoyable hours on "his trail"—or where it was, once upon a time. One of the hikes in my book climbs to the top of Beckwourth Peak, and several trails overlook beautiful Beckwourth Valley, now called Sierra Valley. Another trail looks down on the town of Beckwourth from the top of Sugar Loaf Mountain.

At the end of my hiking book I included a few pages telling a bit about Jim. So, I already knew some of his life story before I started to write this book about him.

I've always loved the history of the old Wild West and have hiked and traveled extensively through much of it. My wife and I spend summers in the Sierra mountains, living in a log house we built a few years ago. Our cabin is only about 15 miles from Jim's old ranch.

I was curious to see the places where Jim had been, so I traveled to various parts of the United States, following Jim's footsteps, hunting for information about him, and taking pictures to use in this book.

For many years I was an adult leader of Boy Scouts, so I've spent plenty of hours hiking and camping with kids. I learned what young adults like to read by being one myself once, raising a couple of my own, and spending trail and camping time with lots of others.

I never had anywhere near as many jobs as Jim had. In fact, I worked for only two different companies. Now I'm retired, so I could spend lots of time doing research about this Wild West superstar.

I went to college at Stanford University near Palo Alto, California. No, I didn't major in English or writing—I graduated in engineering, which doesn't have much to do with writing a book about Jim Beckwourth. However, I figure even engineers can write books, so here's mine. I hope you enjoy reading about Jim.